IMAGES
of America

WILLOW GROVE PARK

In 1916, the overall plan for Willow Grove Park was fairly well fixed. Easton Road ran along the park's eastern side while Old Welsh Road was to the south. Moreland Road cut through the northern section of the park, which extended up to Old York Road where it joined with Easton Road. The trolley terminal was on the piece of land between Easton and Davisville Roads. The traction company's large carbarn was just south of Old York Road. In the early days prior to the terminal, trolley tracks encircled the park. Within the park, the path parallel to Easton Road was known as the Lower or Little Midway. The main concourse within the park along which the major rides were arrayed was called the Midway. As the park developed in the second decade of the 20th century and later, an Upper Midway was formed at the upper end of the Midway running back toward the casino. The casino stood in the center of the park on a knoll. To its north were the park's two lakes with the bandstand off to the eastern side. Walking paths and picnic groves were located throughout. As the park became increasingly dependent on amusement rides for revenues, the outlying pastoral lands were gradually sold off and developed. By the time the park closed in 1976, almost all activity was concentrated around the various Midway concourses.

IMAGES
of America

WILLOW GROVE PARK

Old York Road Historical Society

ARCADIA
PUBLISHING

Published by Arcadia Publishing
Charleston, South Carolina

Library of Congress Catalog Card Number: 2005930929

For all general information contact Arcadia Publishing at:
Telephone 843-853-2070
Fax 843-853-0044
E-mail sales@arcadiapublishing.com
For customer service and orders:
Toll-Free 1-888-313-2665

Visit us on the Internet at www.arcadiapublishing.com

On the cover: A ride on the Alps (previously known as the Mountain Scenic Railway) in one of the ornate roller coaster cars was quite a thrill for these youngsters attending Burk's company picnic on August 7, 1935. Louis Burk, Inc., was founded in 1881 as a manufacturer of Vienna smoked sausages and other meat products and later expanded into a wholesale provision dealer. The firm was located at Third and Girard Streets in Philadelphia. Many people first enjoyed the pleasures of Willow Grove Park while attending one of the many company-sponsored picnics held for employees and their families.

Nothing better symbolizes the essence of Willow Grove Park than a trolley car sporting an advertisement for John Philip Sousa and his band. The park was founded by the People's Traction Company to boost weekend riders on the trolleys. Within 10 years, all lines seemingly converged on Willow Grove. Throughout its heyday, the main attraction of the park was the free public concerts performed daily by the great conductors of the time including Walter Damrosch, Victor Herbert, Patrick Conway, Giuseppe Creatore, Arthur Pryor, and, of course, Sousa.

CONTENTS

PREFACE

The Old York Road Historical Society is pleased to compile and author this history of Willow Grove Park. Much has been said about the park over the years, and several television productions have picked up on the nostalgia for the park, but little has been written in a comprehensive or systematic way. While historian Louis Zanine continues to work on his yet-to-be-published scholarly magnum opus about the park, a book that presents a history of the park through photographs and other images should fill a long-standing gap.

The Old York Road Historical Society was formed in 1936 to study and perpetuate the history and folklore of the communities along and adjacent to the Old York Road from Rising Sun in Philadelphia to New Hope in Bucks County. Over the years, the society has offered a wide variety of programs and scholarly publications covering this area. In its collections, the society has focused primarily on the communities in eastern Montgomery County, specifically the townships of Abington, Cheltenham, Lower Moreland, and Upper Moreland and the boroughs of Bryn Athyn, Hatboro, Jenkintown, and Rockledge. These communities have been covered in the three Arcadia books previously authored by the society, namely, *Abington, Jenkintown, and Rockledge* (2000), *Cheltenham Township* (2001), and *The Morelands and Bryn Athyn* (2002). As with its other three Arcadia publications, the society hopes that this book will help promote and encourage an interest in our local history.

In order to ensure that our collections remain the primary resource for historical study throughout the area, the society is always interested in receiving materials to augment its collections. From photographs and postcards to business records and family manuscripts, the society is able to offer the communities it serves an impressive collection, thanks to the generosity of those who made donations in the past. Any additions you can make to our collections will be well cared for and most appreciated.

Please feel free to visit the society on the Web at www.oyrhs.org or on the lower level of the Jenkintown Library. The archive is open to the public on Mondays from 7:00 to 9:00 p.m., Tuesdays from 11:00 a.m. to 2:00 p.m., Wednesdays from 11:00 a.m. to 3:00 p.m., or by appointment. You may telephone us at 215-886-8590. We hope you enjoy this book, and we appreciate your support.

INTRODUCTION

In order to understand the history of Willow Grove Park, one must start with the history of public transportation in Philadelphia. Since the first immigrants set foot on these shores, people traveled either by foot or by horse. Sometimes the horse pulled a wagon or carriage. During the 1850s, a few entrepreneurs ventured into offering regular public transit for a fee. Along certain roads in the city, a horse-pulled streetcar would travel along tracks in the road. Passengers would pay a few cents for the ride. Soon others entered into the enterprise. Other roads were opened and competition ensued. By the time of the Civil War, the city was awash in private companies ferrying people to and fro. The maintenance of roads, several privately run beginning in the 1830s, was assumed by companies who wanted better routes or to limit the access for competitors.

As Philadelphia grew into a great industrial city following the Civil War, the transit business attracted greater interest. By the late 1880s, various means had been attempted to improve upon the horse-pulled streetcar, but nothing worked until electricity. In December 1892, the Philadelphia Traction Company introduced electric traction on its Catherine and Bainbridge Streets line. Within several years, the city's other horse-drawn streetcar routes were modernized to provide electric trolley service.

By the mid-1890s, there were four major companies that had successfully consolidated the many private transit companies. One of these companies, the People's Traction Company, controlled the route to Willow Grove through its subsidiary, the Philadelphia, Cheltenham and Jenkintown Passenger Railway Company.

The opening of the People's trolley line to Willow Grove on Decoration Day (now Memorial Day) 1895 was a great accomplishment. However, the only one ready for the success of such a development seemed to be Charles Ehrenpfort. His Mineral Springs Park hosted the 10,000 people who came out on the first day of trolley service. From that day on, the crowds only got bigger. Realizing that there was money to be made in offering amusement to the city crowds, the traction company soon was scouting for land. Two farms totaling over 90 acres were purchased, and plans were quickly drawn up and implemented to build a park containing picnic areas, amusements, and a bandstand on beautifully landscaped grounds. Like the Mineral Springs Park, entrance into the park would be free. Food and amusement rides would be available for purchase.

Willow Grove Park opened on Decoration Day 1896 and drew crowds by the thousands. It was estimated that over one million people visited the park during its first season of operation.

Within the year, the People's Traction Company merged into the Union Traction Company controlled by Peter A. B. Widener and William L. Elkins. The Union Traction Company would reincorporate on May 1, 1902, as the Philadelphia Rapid Transit Company (PRT). The company would own and operate the park almost continuously until 1954.

One of the primary goals of the park's management was to provide and maintain a civilized and enlightened cultural atmosphere. From the fine plantings and the electric fountain to standards of dress and decorum regardless of the weather conditions, the park was meant to uplift and edify. All of the amusements were of a character "pleasing to the most refined tastes." The free daily concerts of classical and light classical music performed by the world's top conductors, bands, and orchestras were the culmination of such a philosophy.

In the two decades after the turn of the century, the park witnessed tremendous development, especially in terms of the amusement rides offered. Management spent significant sums of money building new rides and replacing those that had gone out of favor. Most of these rides were located along the Midway, the main avenue within the park. While offering some of the best amusements in the country, the park continued to exact high standards of behavior and decorum from its patrons.

By the time the PRT leased the park to orchestra leader and innovator Meyer Davis in 1926, fundamental changes had occurred in American life that impacted how the park operated. Musical concerts were no longer as popular as they used to be. The automobile was becoming a common sight, and it allowed people to escape even farther from the city, beyond the limited routes of the trolley. In order to bring people to the park, different entertainments were required. During Davis's Roaring Twenties at the park, beauty contests were the norm. Lots of sizzle and swing were called for, and the park tried to deliver. New thrills were needed, and the Thunderbolt was built to satisfy.

However, the onset of the Depression in 1929 triggered by the stock market crash combined with the park's own crash in a December 1929 fire, left Davis with little enthusiasm for the park life. The PRT took back its park and resumed operation. During the 1930s, the park underwent a face lift. New shows were booked and new rides were added. Sleek new roller coaster cars were installed. While the track layout remained the same, the image of the park changed. Throughout the Second World War, the park remained opened, giving area residents a place to go to forget about the fighting for a brief time.

With the return of the troops and the beginnings of the baby boom, the park experienced a renaissance. Attendance, receipts, and profits increased annually. While things were going well for the park, the traction company (known as the Philadelphia Transit Company after 1940) sold it to Baltimore investors in 1954. Additional rides and amusements were added. The day of the amusement park was at its height. People came by car and wanted plenty of diversions and thrills. They did not go away unhappy.

On December 1, 1958, the local Hankin family purchased the park. They would own the facility until its final days. The Hankins focused the park around the Midway and its many rides while starting to develop the surrounding grounds for other commercial uses. As the 1960s wore on, the park went through a slow but steady decline. It was not the place it used to be. To pump new blood and new money into the facility, the Hankins signed a deal with a national amusement company to operate the park in 1971. For four seasons (1972–1975), Six Gun Territory struggled to hold on and ultimately failed. After 80 seasons, the park closed never to reopen. In keeping with the times, the park's land was eventually sold to developers, and a mall was built on the site.

From pleasure park to amusement park to shopping mall with plenty of parking, the grounds of Willow Grove Park over the past 110 years reflect in large part what American society has found to be desirable for its recreation. In some sense, then, the park has not changed much. Regardless of how it has changed, hopefully you will recall your fond memories of Willow Grove Park.

—David B. Rowland, President
Old York Road Historical Society

One

ON THE WAY
TO WILLOW GROVE

In 1891, the Old York Road Passenger Company was founded. In 1893, it became the Philadelphia, Cheltenham and Jenkintown Passenger Railway Company with the goal to build a trolley line to Willow Grove based on the newly successful technology of electrically powered streetcars. A major generating plant was built in Ogontz on Old York Road. The construction of the line was a major undertaking. Essentially the old road was dug up so that the electric power and tracks could be laid down. This image shows the Ogontz Power Plant to the left and the Shoemaker Mill on the right, both on what is now Church Road, which used to be Old York Road prior to the cut-through in the mid-1940s. The picture, looking south, dates from late 1893.

The Ogontz Power Plant was built in a Spanish style of yellow brick with a tiled roof. The trolley was built to Jenkintown by the winter of 1894 and extended to Willow Grove in the spring of 1895. Originally Old York Road ran around Ogontz Hill along the route of Church Road and the Old York Road Spur. At the beginning of World War II, Old York Road was targeted by the military for modernization and the cut-through was ordered. The line up Old York Road stopped running in September 1940, and the power plant was soon demolished for the Old York Road cut-through.

Three huge 1,200-horsepower Allis-Corliss engines powered the Ogontz Power Station. In addition, there were five generators producing a total of 2,800 kilowatts of power. Nine 250-horsepower Berry boilers were also employed. The condensing water was cooled by forcing it through spray nozzles arrayed along the Tookany Creek, which ran behind the power plant.

The Willow Grove Power Plant was located at what is now the northeast corner of Moreland and Easton Roads. Willow Grove was a direct current generating station. In 1904, the station was expanded to include a substation for alternating current, connecting with the Glenside substation. By 1905 (when pictured), the power plant had six engines running at a combined 2,050 horsepower and six generators producing 1,350 kilowatts of power. The substation provided an additional 1,000 kilowatts. The electricity produced not only powered the trolleys but also ran the park rides and lights.

The Car Barn, pictured here in 1920 but not much changed from the time of its construction in 1895, housed the trolley cars when they were not running. The building was constructed by Charles M. McCaul, who also built the Reading Terminal in Philadelphia. The building faced toward Old York Road and ran parallel to Davisville and Easton Roads.

A Trolley Trip on Old York Pike to Willow Grove Park

While the ride to Willow Grove might seem an uneventful trip to modern-day readers, the trip in 1896 from the city to the country was touted as being equal to a day at the park. The trip from center city Philadelphia was one hour and 20 minutes and cost 15¢ one way (5¢ for each of the three zones). Guidebooks were published to point out the sites one would encounter along the journey. Conductors were educated about important landmarks and would identify them to the passengers. It is important to keep in mind that most Philadelphians had never been out of the city. The trip, then, was cause for both great excitement and some degree of seriousness to make the excursion not only pleasurable but also edifying. This guidebook was published in 1896 by the Union Traction Company for the "suburban excursionist" and details the sites on the way to Willow Grove. Not only the guidebooks but also the various instruments of the press described in great detail the journey to Willow Grove and the care taken in getting people there by the most pleasurable means. Old York Road was improved throughout and described as a "magnificent serpent-like boulevard sixteen miles in length, hard and smooth, kept in perfect state by a large force of men, and forming a panorama of rare rural scenery." Steamrollers were used to keep the road smooth, and electric sprinklers were run to dampen the road, thus keeping the dust down. The remainder of this chapter is devoted primarily to a tour up the Old York Road, viewing the sites that were identified in various guidebooks as being worthy of one's attention.

The Widener Memorial Industrial Training School for Crippled Children was located on a 32-acre tract at the intersection of Broad Street and Olney Avenue. Peter A. B. Widener founded the school in 1902 as a memorial to his late wife, Hannah Josephine. Once admitted to the school, children were given the best medical and surgical care available and were educated in a trade of their choosing. The building was designed by Philadelphia architect Horace Trumbauer, who also built Widener's palatial home, Lynnewood Hall, in Elkins Park.

Looking south on Old York Road from Olney Avenue, the property of the Jewish Hospital is beyond the trolley on the left. The hospital, founded in 1865 in West Philadelphia, relocated to its present site in 1873. The ground was originally a part of Swarthmore, the country estate of Thomas Morris. The Widener School is on the right behind the wall. The institute building was eventually demolished, but the signature wall still remains. At the time of the photograph, Broad Street (on the right) was only completed up to Olney Avenue.

On the northwest corner of Old York Road and Olney Avenue was Butler Place, the 107-acre estate of Pierce Butler. Originally built by Matthew Ingram in 1791, the mansion was sold to Francis Breuil in 1802. Breuil was a powder agent in Philadelphia and had many business transactions with E. I. Dupont de Nemours and Company. In 1810, the property was sold to Maj. Pierce Butler, an esteemed member of the Continental Congress and signer of the U.S. Constitution. Butler's son married the celebrated British actress Fanny Kemble. The estate was later the home of Owen Wister, well-known author of *The Virginian*.

Joseph Wharton, descended from Thomas Wharton who came to America in 1683, was an industrialist, scientist, and philanthropist. He also founded the Wharton School of Business at the University of Pennsylvania and cofounded the Bethlehem Steel Company. Several generations of his family lived at Ontalauna, a French Second Empire–style mansion. The home was constructed around 1880 and was located west of Old York Road between Milestown and Branchtown at what today would be the intersection of Chelten Avenue and Sydenham Street.

Silver Pine Farm, the ancestral home of the DeBenneville family, was located on Old York Road in Branchtown, west of Broad Street. The farmhouse was built in 1746 and was named for the silver pine trees planted on the lawn. With forefathers from a prominent French Huguenot family, George DeBenneville was a well-known preacher while a relative, Dr. Daniel DeBenneville, was a surgeon in the Continental Army. The home was alternately the headquarters of Washington and Cornwallis during the Battle of Germantown.

The City Line Tavern was located at the southeast corner of City Line (now Cheltenham Avenue) and Old York Road. The hotel was constructed about 1800 by Joseph Rorer for the accommodation of local farmers bringing produce to Philadelphia from Bucks and Montgomery Counties. Rorer was a soldier in the Continental Army and was an eyewitness at the Battle of Germantown.

Roadside was the home of Quaker abolitionist Lucretia Mott from 1857 until the time of her death in 1880. Sited on an eight-acre tract of land, the three-story stone farmhouse was built in 1753 with an addition in 1757. Edward Morris Davis, Mott's son-in-law, purchased the property in 1854. Mott and Davis were both founders of the Philadelphia Anti-Slavery Society and were active in the establishment of the Underground Railroad. In 1911, builder William T. B. Roberts demolished the home for the development of Latham Park.

Idro, the summer home of hat manufacturer John Batterson Stetson, was located on the west side of Old York Road, north of Juniper Avenue in Elkins Park. Constructed in the late 1880s, the architect of the original structure is believed to be George T. Pearson. Along with other architects, he returned several times for alterations and additions to the rambling French chateau–style mansion. The 15-acre estate also contained a large stable, a conservatory, two rose houses, and its own power plant for steam and electricity.

16

Originally named Shoemakertown, the small village at the intersection of Old York and Church Roads was founded around the Shoemaker Mill that stood along the Tookany Creek. In 1888, the town changed its name to Ogontz in deference to Jay Cooke and his estate of that name. Looking south on Old York Road from the Ogontz Power House, the building on the left with the tower and awning was the Ogontz Hotel run by Alfred Tyson. Built in 1856, the structure was an unusual combination of Second Empire and stick-style architecture. Next to the hotel was the Cheltenham Coach Works, run by George W. Moore and Horace Ervien, makers of wagons, carriages, and buggies. Both buildings were demolished in 1970 for Cheltenham Township's Ogontz urban renewal project.

At the top of Ogontz Hill sat the elegant mansions of George Sidney Fox and his two sons, Caleb Fellows Fox and Frederick Morton Fox. George Fox was a director of the Union Traction Company and, along with his two sons, was involved in street railway finance. The Foxes also worked closely with Peter A. B. Widener and William L. Elkins in the competitive promotion of streetcar lines throughout Philadelphia. Shown is Foxholm, Frederick's home. All three homes were designed in the 1880s by the celebrated architectural firm Furness and Evans. In the mid-1940s, the Fox estates were demolished for the cut-through of Old York Road.

One of the most spectacular properties for travelers on the way to Willow Grove Park was Lindenhurst, the 108-acre estate of John Wanamaker located at the southwest corner of Old York and Township Line Roads. Wanamaker had department stores in New York and Paris as well as his main store in center city Philadelphia. While serving as postmaster general, Wanamaker entertained Pres. Benjamin Harrison here in 1889. Built in 1883, the home was consumed by a disastrous fire in February 1907. A new mansion was later built on the site. Unfortunately for many summertime trolley passengers, there was not a good view of the house from the street as the home was well protected by a buffer of trees and shrubs that surrounded the property.

18

The land above the Wanamaker estate was rather open country. This view looks northeast across Old York Road near Wyncote Road. Off to the right and beyond the fields is the Abington Friends Meeting. In 1697, Abington Friends established a meetinghouse and school near Washington Lane. The school was the only institution of higher learning along Old York Road for many years.

This view looking south on Old York Road above West Avenue shows several hotels and important enterprises in the heart of Jenkintown. From its beginnings, Old York Road was a vital route, and Jenkintown an important stop, for travelers coming to and from Philadelphia. The building on the far left with the awning and carriage out front is the Cottman House. The building diagonally opposite on the southwest corner of Old York Road and West Avenue is the Jenkintown Hotel. Although both businesses had excellent food and lodging for trolley passengers and other wayfarers, the Cottman House also had a large livery stable and held well-attended horse auctions.

19

In 1896, the newly formed Huntingdon Valley Country Club purchased the Noble farm and converted the residence into a clubhouse and the farm into a golf course. The property was located on the east side of Old York Road above what is now the Fairway. Dating from the early 19th century, the farmhouse was the residence of Samuel Noble, who was later president of the Jenkintown National Bank. During the later years of his engagements at Willow Grove Park, John Philip Sousa resided at the club and stabled his horses in the barn. Walter Damrosch also resided at the club and frequently entertained there.

The wooded estate on the left, as well as the stone farmhouse on the opposite side of Old York Road, belonged to artist John Lambert Jr. The residence, Aysgarth, still stands and is located just below the Abington Free Library. The farmhouse had previously belonged to the Dillon family. It was demolished in the 1920s for a new residence. A medical office building at the corner of Brook Road now stands here. The steeple is that of Abington Presbyterian Church. The church was rebuilt in 1896, a year after it burned in a devastating fire.

Folly Farms was near the intersection of Old York and Edge Hill Roads in Abington. The ground was originally part of the property of John Barclay Stevenson Jr. In February 1909, the Elkins family purchased the 107-acre farm. Over the years, Folly Farms became known for the excellence of its merchandise, milk deliveries, and horse auctions. In 1920, the family sold the property to William Davidson, who renamed it Brentwood Farms. In 1952–1953, the grounds were sold for development. Despite a fire in 1956, the original farmhouse still serves as a rectory for Our Lady Help of Christians Roman Catholic Church.

Approaching Willow Grove from the south, travelers came upon the Fountain House Inn with its double front porch. Founded before 1717, the inn was also known for a time as the Willow Grove Hotel. At its height, it boasted 18 rooms, each with a fireplace and oak floors. The inn was demolished in 1961. The sheds also belonged to the inn. The house across the street belonged to Dr. Franklin Watson and was located between Cherry and Church Streets.

In 1897, a traction line from Willow Grove to Doylestown was built along the Willow Grove and Doylestown Turnpike (now Easton Road), with the first trolley arriving in Doylestown in May 1898. In 1900, the mortgage on this line was foreclosed and purchased by George D. Widener and William H. Shelmerdine, who soon moved control of the line to their Union Traction Company. In 1901, a spur off of the Doylestown line was built into Hatboro. Both lines operated until February 14, 1931, when bus service fully replaced the trolleys (express bus service had been in operation since 1927). The origins of Doylestown go back to 1745 when William Doyle built a tavern at the crossroads of two major highways in Bucks County. Over time, a village was established around the tavern. Its central location in Bucks County eventually made Doylestown a commercial and cultural focal point for the region, and the borough was incorporated in 1838.

The village of Edison was located in southern Doylestown Township where Easton Road crossed the Neshaminy Creek. The first bridge over the creek was built in the 1760s. In 1880, a post office was established and named after Thomas Edison. Turk was a village very close to Edison, and many times the two villages were considered one. This view from 1906 shows the Old Turk's Head Tavern on Easton Road beside the trolley line. The tavern was demolished around 1918.

The Horsham Friends Meeting was founded in 1717. The following year, Hannah Carpenter deeded a 50-acre tract of land for a meetinghouse. The present meetinghouse dates from 1803. At that time, Friends also provided the first schooling in Horsham Township.

Approaching Willow Grove from the north on Easton Road, this view toward the town was taken on Easton Road at Summit Avenue. The homes on the left are at Lakeview Avenue. Down Easton Road on the right, the first property is on Center Avenue. There was only one track on the trolley line to Doylestown.

The traction line from Wayne Junction and Germantown to Willow Grove through Glenside was completed in 1904. Upon leaving Philadelphia, passengers taking the trolley would pass Grey Towers, the 138-acre estate of William Welsh Harrison, who was president of the Franklin Sugar Company. Modeled on Alnwick Castle in England, the castlelike structure was designed by Horace Trumbauer in 1893. It contained 41 rooms and was built of Chestnut Hill grey stone and Indiana limestone. Beaver College purchased the property in 1929, and in 2000, the school changed its name to Arcadia University.

This woodland view looks south from Church Road toward Limekiln Pike over the 110-acre Endsmeet Farm, the estate of Anna Wharton and Harrison Smith Morris. Today Panther Road in Wyncote cuts through here. A large portion of the farm became the site of Cheltenham High School, which was built in 1959.

The Glenside substation was built in 1904 as part of the Philadelphia Rapid Transit Company's adoption of alternating current. The station had a 2,000-kilowatt capacity. The building is now owned by Arcadia University and is located on Church Road east of Limekiln Pike.

This view along Keswick Avenue at the intersection of Waverly Road looks north with New Road going off to the left. In the 1920s, developer William T. B. Roberts built Craftsman-style homes on the ground directly ahead, and the Glenside Memorial Hall was built on the right. The two signs advertise Ardsley Burial Park. The one on the left reads, "There is comfort and profit both to be gained by purchasing NOW an Ardsley Burial Park plot." The sign in the center states, "When the crepe is on the door is not the time to wisely choose the family's final resting place." One would hope that this was not a forewarning concerning the safety of the rides at the park.

Trolleys going north on Keswick Avenue proceeded through the development of Roslyn Terrace. The homes pictured in the foreground are at Keswick and Menlo Avenues. Roslyn Terrace was one of a number of planned communities William T. B. Roberts built. Roberts also was the one who convinced Peter A. B. Widener and William L. Elkins to run a traction line through Glenside. He worked closely with Widener and Elkins in the subdivision and improvement of many suburban properties all through Abington and Cheltenham Townships. It was not at all unusual for the traction companies (or their owners) to have a financial interest in the undeveloped lands through which the trolleys ran.

After making a graceful left turn from Keswick Avenue, trolley cars paralleled Jenkintown Road briefly then made a right onto Tyson Avenue. This view from 1907 looks north on Tyson Avenue near Custer Avenue. The grove of trees to the left obscures the grounds of Hillside Cemetery, chartered in 1890.

Two

BEGINNINGS
1895–1904

With the advent of streetcar service to Willow Grove on Decoration Day 1895, Mineral Springs Park proved to be the only attraction for those Philadelphians wishing to spend a summer's day in the rural and cool climes of Willow Grove. The Mineral Springs Inn originated as a tavern licensed in 1803 by George Rex. Charles Ehrenpfort purchased the property in 1890 for $17,900.

In early 1892, Charles Ehrenpfort began extensive work on the grounds adjoining his Mineral Springs Inn to transform it into a fine pleasure ground for picnics and excursions. A 10-acre lake was formed by damming up the stream that flowed from the mineral springs. The Mineral Springs was rich in iron and had long been famous for its beneficial qualities. On the lake, a variety of boats were provided and one could also fish. In the winter, skaters took advantage of the frozen lake.

MINERAL SPRINGS HOTEL
WILLOW GROVE, PA.

LUNCHEON 65c
Served from 12 to 2 P. M.

English Beef Soup, Consomme
or Tomato Juice

Deviled Crab, Cole Slaw
Hamburger Steak
Roast Leg of Lamb
Cold Sugar-Cured Ham, Potato Salad

Browned New Potato   Fresh String Beans
Sugar Corn   French Fried Potatoes

Home-Made Pie or Ice Cream

Rolls and Butter   Coffee

Surrounding the lake, walkways were laid out and a number of trees were planted. Grounds were set aside for croquet, lawn tennis, and baseball. A large carousel was installed and there were also swings, a shooting gallery, and a 10-pin alley. There was ample capacity for large crowds with picnic tables and benches. There was also a kitchen for cooking and various pavilions and shelters to protect people from the rain. The park was served by the Reading Railroad, which passed through Willow Grove. A boardwalk connected the park with the station, and special excursion rates were offered. The park aimed to cater to Sunday schools, church festivals, picnics, and social and family parties. Management made it clear that any rough or boisterous elements would not be allowed, and the attendants on duty were trained to serve as police officers if need be. The park promised that no intoxicating beverages would be allowed or sold on the park grounds (as distinguished from inside the hotel and restaurant, where liquor was available). Anticipating the inauguration of trolley service, Ehrenpfort had architect Horace Trumbauer do major renovations to the hotel for the 1895 season. An addition was added to the main building that included a ballroom, a new kitchen, and a large dining room. A menu from the Mineral Springs Hotel would have been for those who could afford the fine dining. Popcorn cakes, ice cream, and lemonade were also sold on the grounds.

Initially the inn was the only establishment in Willow Grove to offer alcohol. By a shrewd business deal, a prior owner of the inn, John Berrell, had purchased the only other tavern in town, the Red Lion Inn, for the sole purpose of relinquishing its liquor license, thus giving his Mineral Springs a monopoly on "wet" refreshment. Soon after Willow Grove Park opened, however, other establishments sprang up and applied for licenses. This was convenient for people like Sousa, who stayed at the hotel during his first few years while at Willow Grove.

In 1912, Charles Ehrenpfort sold the Mineral Springs to his son Frederick. The following year, major renovations were again done on the inn. The interior was gutted, and a new lobby was created. The old porches were also removed, and new front and southern porches were added. The hotel operated until the family sold the business in 1926. The inn was demolished in January 1938. The hotel was located on the ground where the present-day Bally Fitness Spa is located on Old York Road, just where Old York and Easton Roads diverge going north.

With the resounding success of the trolley line to Willow Grove, the owners of the People's Traction Company soon set about to find a suitable site for their own park. Two parcels of land were secured. The first, a 10-acre parcel owned by John Cadwalader, was located just south of Old York Road and extended down to Moreland Road (then known as the New Welsh Road). The second, an 82-acre farm owned by William C. Newport, was located on the west side of Easton Road (then known as the Germantown and Willow Grove Turnpike) between Moreland and Old Welsh Roads. Work began almost immediately on the construction of the park. However, by the early months of 1896, work was running behind schedule. The work force was increased to nearly 500 men (mostly Italian), and the park was ready for opening day on Decoration Day 1896. This view was taken on August 2, 1896, and shows the newly completed park in the distance. Moreland Road runs east into the distance. On the north side of the road, to the left in the foreground, is the farm of George R. Berrell. Beyond the farm, the trolley car shed is visible. On higher ground above the car shed are the newly built homes owned by David Cherry. On the south side of Moreland Road is the farm of William Kimball. In 1906, the park would first

lease and later purchase a portion of the Kimball farm for expansion. Beyond and to the south of the grove of trees is the casino, set on the knoll where the old Paul mansion previously stood. The mansion contained 19 rooms and was originally intended to be the centerpiece of the park. However, it was realized that the renovations required to convert the house into a restaurant would be too much, and so the decision was made to raze the mansion and build a new casino. The park was designed by civil engineers Chester E. Albright and Herman Wendell with the firm of Wendell and Smith Corporation. Albright would later go on to form the Philadelphia Toboggan Company (PTC) with Henry Auchy. The PTC made amusement rides not only for Willow Grove but also for many other amusement parks throughout the country. The overall design concept was to be an Italian effect with Colonial architecture. All the initial buildings on the property were designed by architect Horace Trumbauer. Trumbauer had recently made his name among wealthy Philadelphians with the design of William Welsh Harrison's Grey Towers. He would eventually become one of the most important architects in the country.

The official entrance to Willow Grove Park was on Old York Road. At the entrance stood a brownstone lodge that served as both the administrative offices of the park as well as the home of its superintendent, the first being McClellan Hersh. Hersh oversaw the park's 150 employees. Like the Mineral Springs, the park was open to the public free of charge. At the outset, the park was considered "the finest pleasure park in America."

The farmlands were transformed into a bucolic setting with the finest plantings. The Philadelphia Hedge Company planted 750 trees, 3,500 assorted shrubbery, 4,000 privet plants for hedges, 1,000 honeysuckles, 500 roses, and 5,000 bedding plants. Numerous decorative plants and palms, some of which were the largest ones available, were also brought in. The central vista lay between the lodge entrance and the casino, with groupings of trees to either side. The lily pond was a unique feature containing over 1,500 aquatic plants, among which were many rare lilies. A rustic red granite bridge and other small pavilions also decorated the northern section of the park.

Originally, the trolley turned off of Old York Road and made a complete circuit of the park. There were various points along the route where passengers could disembark. The trolley would then exit the park at the same point at which it had entered.

In addition to the trolley lines that served Willow Grove Park, the Pennsylvania and Reading Railroad also provided transit to the park. Trains through Willow Grove ran on regular schedules, while special excursion trains were added on weekends. The Reading regularly brought people to Willow Grove from points throughout eastern Pennsylvania including Harrisburg, Hershey, Lebanon, Reading, Robesonia, Pottstown, Royersford, and Phoenixville. Willow Grove, indeed, was a destination for people from far and wide.

The Band Shell contained offices and dressing rooms in addition to the main performing stage. The shell itself was 40 feet tall and 50 feet in diameter with an apron for soloists that ran across the entire length of the stage. Massive Ionic columns framed the structure. Frederick N. Innes, one of the most celebrated bandmasters of the age, had submitted plans for the building. The acoustic properties of the shell were considered perfect, the most delicate notes being plainly heard in all parts of the grove. In fact, it was said that the music could be heard for miles around. A large awning shaded the platform from the afternoon sun.

During the first year and for 30 years thereafter, one of the principal attractions of the park was the free public concerts. Park management contracted performers of the highest caliber, and there was not an evening during the summer season in Willow Grove, weather permitting, without live music. Concerts were held twice a day during the season, one in the afternoon and another at night. Thousands gathered daily for the musical events, and seating was often hard to find. During the early years, benches were arranged up the side of the hill toward the casino.

The New
Willow Grove Park
(In the Chelten Hills)

FESTIVAL CONCERTS BY
INNES And His Famous Fifty.
Saturday, August 8, 1896.

The first year's musical concerts belonged solely to Frederick N. Innes and his "Famous Fifty." Innes was born in London, England, on October 29, 1854. His early musical training was in the band of Her Majesty's First Life Guard. He was a skilled trombone player and came to be considered the world's greatest. While still in England, he conceived of the idea of a military band organized for concert purposes only, and he was able to organize such a group in San Francisco in 1887. Innes met with such success that he was offered the leadership of the 13th Regiment Band of New York. His stature in the field was unmatched. At Willow Grove, his concerts were so successful that the season was extended two weeks until September 20. Concert programs contained a mix of classical music, operatic selections, marches, songs, and lighter classics. Monday night was public request night, and Friday evenings were strictly classical nights. On September 19, Innes premiered his own composition, *Willow Grove*, the first of many works dedicated to the park or its patrons. Famous soloists of the day frequently appeared with the band. For many people, the concerts would be their first exposure to live classical music. For the park planners, the concerts stood as their greatest achievement in promoting an "air of refinement."

Initially there were three lakes in the park, the largest covering four acres with a depth ranging from two to six feet. Near the center of the lake was the great electric fountain, inaugurated during a special concert on the Fourth of July 1896 at 9:00 p.m. Designed by electrical engineer F. W. Darlington, the fountain cost $100,000 to build. It was 44 feet wide with two tiered basins rising above the lake and 867 water jets. The fountain played in the afternoon and evening, in conjunction with the adjoining concerts. An electric motor allowed the 12 main waterlines feeding the fountain to be operated independently, thus allowing for a level of control over the fountain display never before possible. There were various formations that the fountain could produce, including sheaves of wheat, a cone with smaller wheat sheaves inside, vases, a ring, and big and little fans.

The fountain was illuminated by 15 lamps and was the first fully electric fountain, being operated, pumped, and lit entirely by electricity. Nighttime illuminations were very popular and were occasionally enhanced with fireworks. The nighttime combination of the fountain, well-lit buildings, and strings of electric lights strung between trees and around buildings made Willow Grove Park "Philadelphia's Fairyland."

Located on the shore of the lake, the Fountain House contained the controls of the fountain and access to the fountain itself. The structure would become one of the most recognized features of the park and one of the longest lived. Indeed, it is the pavilion of the fountain house that later became the logo for the Willow Grove Park Mall. The building echoed the features of the casino in its design. Within this building, a man would operate the controls for the fountain's water jets. An arched tunnel ran under the lake to the fountain, allowing an operator to control the fountain's colored lights. Powerful lights were directed up through heavy glass discs to the water above. Each disc was capped by a rotary table containing colored glass, and by rotating the glass, the fountain was made to appear blue, green, yellow, violet, and all shades of the rainbow.

The second largest lake, which adjoined the main lake, contained a boat launch where patrons could rent a rowboat. For those who wished for the boating experience without the exertion, an electric launch also ran throughout the day. The lakes were fed by springs that were present on the original farmland. A stream had also run through the farm.

The Willow Grove Park Casino was the central building of the park. The term "casino," prior to its current meaning as strictly a gambling place, referred to a social gathering site where one might dance, listen to music, or gamble. At the park, the casino was used exclusively as a café. The structure was painted yellow and white, colors that were used in all the park's buildings and that gave a rich tone to the entire architecture. Awnings shaded porches when the light was strong.

The building's piazza was the fashionable spot for dining. The rotunda served as a dining room during inclement weather. Fine views of the park grounds were afforded from all sides, as the casino stood on the knoll. During the park's first year, the casino quickly grew to serve 500 people at a time. There were 33 well-trained waiters with an additional 10 on the weekends. The casino's a la carte menu contained a great variety of summer dishes.

In order to keep the quality of the park at its highest, standards of decorum and dress were strictly enforced by a contingent of park guards, initially 17 in number, under Capt. Robert L. Williams. Clad in gray uniforms, it was said of the guards, "They are, every one of them, intelligent, manly fellows." It was very important to management that there were no problems, for the park was touted as being safe for unaccompanied ladies with children. During the first year, there was never an arrest or cause for an arrest within the park.

In olden times, ladies normally had their own place of repose while out in public. Banks, stores, and other respectable establishments all had a ladies' section, where women could retreat from the men. Willow Grove Park was no different, and the original Ladies' Pavilion was located on the ground centered between the Midway and the casino. The building contained washrooms, closets, and nicely furnished lavatories for women and children.

The Shoot-the-Chutes was one of the more vigorous amusements in the park. Touted as the most up-to-date in America, the ride took advantage of the third lake in the park that was located along Easton Road. For the ride, passengers would get into a boat, which would then ascend a tower to the top of a chute. The boat would then slide down into the lake, causing a bit of a splash, but not so much as to muss fine Sunday dresses. An adjoining pavilion allowed the less adventurous to view the proceedings. The ride cost $40,000 to construct and was similar to one in Atlantic City. The ride was removed after the 1904 season.

The Biograph Theatre was built as a movie house, the first building in the world built solely for the purpose of showing moving pictures. The movie projector, called a vitascope, realistically produced living pictures and scenes. Moving pictures had only been developed within the year, and the first public demonstration of Edison's vitascope occurred just months before in New York City on April 23, 1896. Also in the building were phonographs and graphophones that both played musical rolls as well as kinetoscopes and x-rays.

During the 1890s, the nation was in the grip of a bicycling craze. One of the park's first rides was the Bicycle Swing, a ride similar to a merry-go-round in which bicycles were each attached to an overhead trolley. The park also had a quarter-mile, beautifully banked bicycle track that was free to cyclers. There was a grandstand facing the track that contained dressing and washrooms below. To prepare for the track at Willow Grove, the park sent experts all over the country to examine the best bicycle tracks. The new track was considered one of the finest built for cycling.

The Scenic Railway was the first roller coaster ride at the park and was the longest lived, still in operation at the time of the park's close. The ride took passengers up to the tops of the trees and then a quarter mile out into the tree grove. The turns were gradual, and there were just a few slight dips. The coaster utilized side friction, where the wheels locked around the rail to keep the cars on the track. The ride cost 5¢ and was popularly known as the "Nickel Scenic." In 1901, the entrance pavilion was doubled in size and more trains were added.

When the park opened, it had a carousel built by the E. Joy Morris Carousel Company of Philadelphia. The carousel house was designed and built by the carousel company as well and matched in style carousel houses throughout the nation. The ride at Willow Grove was considered one of the best and safest in the country. The Morris ride remained at the park until it was replaced at the end of the 1905 season.

Carousel carving was something of a high art form. Many of the best artisans were German immigrants who had settled in the Germantown section of Philadelphia. The animals were expertly carved and beautifully painted, thus greeting eager riders with an overwhelming sense of the fantastic. Classical music accompanied the merry-go-round on its ride. The Morris firm produced about two dozen carousels from 1896 to 1904 before the company was sold to the Philadelphia Toboggan Company.

While the casino offered fine dining for those of financial means, the vast majority of people who came to the park did so to picnic in the park's three picnic groves. Grove No. 1 was near the main entrance, Grove No. 2 was in the middle of the park, and Grove No. 3 was in the upper (southwest) corner. In total, the groves could accommodate 25,000 people.

Each grove contained 30 to 50 tables with benches, adapted especially for picnic purposes. Each picnic grove also contained hydrants that provided plenty of fresh water. There were also kitchens in each grove with hot water. The kitchens were located in large frame buildings and were equipped with stoves and kitchen utensils. All the facilities were freely accessible to the public without charge.

Built in 1897 for the park's second season, the Mystic Moorish Maze (later simply the Mirror Maze) contained a maze of confusing halls and mirrors that proved challenging to navigate and distorted one's image. Located on the Midway, the building was totally remodeled in 1901, eliminating the Moorish effect. In order to make way for Venice, the building was relocated in 1907 to a site along the Little Midway.

In 1897, the bicycle craze was still going strong, and the park greatly expanded the seating capacity of the bicycle track. Bicycle meets were frequently held, and handsome prizes were awarded. For a time, the park's track held the world record for the one mile at one minute and 35 seconds. The craze did not last forever, and the track was removed after the 1899 season. The main grandstand was retained and overlooked a new baseball diamond. Additional athletic fields were also built, as were lawn tennis courts and a cricket field.

In 1897, park management took a daring risk and hired Walter Damrosch and his New York Symphony Orchestra to provide music for the season. Some felt that an orchestra was not suited for outdoor concerts and that it would not draw the crowds. Advocates felt that a fine orchestra would not only give Willow Grove a prestige that no other park enjoyed but, through the medium of good music, would attract people who could and would spend money. Damrosch proved wildly popular. He set a new standard for outdoor summer music in America and stimulated a popular appreciation of classical music. The founding of the Philadelphia Orchestra in 1901 would be attributable in part to the popularity Damrosch had brought to symphonic music. Other summer parks all over the country picked up on the success at Willow Grove and soon offered similar concerts. Like Innes, Damrosch gave two daily concerts; Monday was a complete symphony, and Friday was Wagner night.

Season 1899.

Willow Grove Park
(In the Chelten Hills)

DAILY CONCERTS BY

Walter Damrosch and his Famous **Orchestra**

Afternoon and Evening.

WILLOW GROVE MARCH

AS PLAYED BY

THE BANDA ROSSA

BY

EUGENIO SORRENTINO.

PIANO .... .50
4 HANDS .... .75
BAND 1.00

Philadelphia.
Theodore Presser.
1798 Chestnut Str.

While Damrosch proved a success, Thomas Brooke and his Chicago Marine Band had already been contracted for the 1898 season. However, in 1899, Damrosch returned and a policy was adopted of having both orchestras and bands play every season. Included in the 1899 musical season was Eugenio Sorrentino and his Italian band, Banda Rossa, so named for their red hats. Sorrentino was also a composer as well as conductor, and his *Willow Grove March* premiered on May 27.

45

For the 1900 season, park management decided to erect a large pavilion abutting the music shell for the purpose of keeping performances running and audiences sheltered from afternoon showers. The Music Pavilion contained seating for 4,000 people. Damrosch helped to plan the building, wanting to prevent the music from floating away into the upper air. On July 12, 1902, a large crowd gathered under the pavilion to hear a concert by the Kilties. The Kilties Band of Canada was a world famous band from Belleville, Ontario, and was under the direction of William F. Robinson.

John Philip Sousa and his band made their first appearance at Willow Grove Park during the 1901 season. Their inaugural concert was on Decoration Day when Sousa introduced his new march "The Invincible Eagle." Sousa was born in 1854 in Washington, D.C. By the time he was 13, Sousa was serving as an apprentice in the United States Marine Band playing the trombone. He also became an accomplished violin player. In 1876, Sousa came to Philadelphia to play violin in the Centennial Exposition Orchestra. He stayed in town for four years before returning to Washington where he was appointed director of the Marine Band by Marine Corps commandant Charles G. McCawley (who, incidentally, is buried in the Abington Presbyterian Church Cemetery). In 1892, Sousa left to form his own band, which toured the United States and Europe with great success. Known as the "March King," Sousa was a gifted composer as well, writing over 100 works. Over the years, Sousa would either premiere, compose, or complete many of his best compositions at Willow Grove Park. He came to epitomize the refinement the park embodied and all that the park meant to those who remembered the days when he played there. Sousa proved to be the greatest draw the park had, as evidenced by the crowds who gathered for this opening day concert in 1902.

46

In this *c.* 1902 photograph one gets a sense of the pastoral nature of the park with its well-maintained, landscaped grounds, the fountain and lake, and the bucolic setting of the Music Pavilion by the side of the lake. Running across the picture and bounded by hedges is Moreland Road, which shows no signs of traffic. People simply walked along the path and through the hedges to get to the other side. The trolley car is taking its route along the perimeter of the grounds. A few large homes set along the hill overlook the southeastern corner of the park. While the lake and its surroundings served as the main focus of the park in the early days, within a few years, the addition of other amusements and roller coasters would begin a slow shift of attention away from the pastoral toward the more thrilling.

Ye Olde Mill was an amusement ride built in 1901 next to the original Morris carousel on the Midway. The ride operated through the end of the 1908 season and over its years was modified and improved several times. One sat in an upholstered boat and passed through a narrow canal or millrace. As the boat made its journey, various scenes would be illuminated, including a scene of Old Christ Church, a moonlit view of the Schuylkill River from the Girard Avenue Bridge, scenes copied from Dore of Dante's *Inferno,* and the bathing hour at the Atlantic City beach. The scenic effects were all artistically executed and quite elaborate.

Built in 1902, the Fairy Theatre was located between the Biograph Theatre to the left and the Ye Olde Mill to the right. It was the largest structure on the park grounds. At the time, the theater was touted as the latest thing in the amusement line. A form of eye lens was attached to each seat, and as viewers looked through the lens, full-grown actors would appear as small fairies. The theater sat 200 to 300 people. Various scenes and tales were acted out, including *Jack and the Bean Stalk,* and a maypole dance was performed. The theater proved to be a failure and closed after the 1902 season.

In 1902, a second carousel was added at the eastern end of the Midway. The carousel was made by the Dentzel Company of Philadelphia. The ride had assorted animals and was fitted with a mechanical device to give them a lifelike motion, a novelty at the time. Founded by Gustav A. Dentzel, the firm was known for its realistic reproductions and wide variety of animals. The firm remained a family affair for two generations before being sold to the Philadelphia Toboggan Company in 1929.

At nighttime, the carousel, like all the other buildings in the park, was illuminated by hundreds of electric lights. The Dentzel carousel would remain at the park through the 1909 season before it was withdrawn and replaced with another carousel.

Also in 1902, the wooden lakeside lunch pavilion, known as the Light Luncheon Pavilion, was greatly enlarged with a stone addition and was renamed the Lakeside Café. It could accommodate over 500 people. The food served was more moderately priced than the casino.

The Lakeside Café proved to be a hit with the children. The park catered to Sunday school groups and others who wanted a conducive atmosphere in which to gather or go for a visit. Annually the park sponsored a Children's Day, which brought the little ones out in droves. There was also an official Sunday School Day instituted in 1903.

In addition to special days for the children, family reunions like the Carrell family reunion and organization reunions or gatherings were regularly held at the park. Specific days would be given over to various themes, which were also reflected in the musical programming. There was a Welsh Day, Medical Day, Catholic Abstainer's Day (sponsored by the Catholic Total Abstinence Union of Philadelphia), German-American Night, Christian Endeavor Day, and National Orphans' Day, among others. Various school reunions were also regularly held at the park.

1711·1902.

FIRST RE-UNION

OF THE

DESCENDENTS

OF

James and Dinah Carrell,

AT

WILLOW GROVE PARK,

WILLOW GROVE, PA.

On Saturday, September 13th, 1902.

Order of Exercises:

Meet at 10 A. M.

Reception Committee introducing kin to kin.

Handing family records to the secretary and registering names and addresses.

At noon the conch shell will be blown for dinner.

On July 25, 1903, the Grand Army of the Republic of Philadelphia and Vicinity held its annual reunion at the park. The group was composed of Union Civil War veterans. There were demonstrations and a campfire, and many veterans attended the festivities. The Grand Army of the Republic gathered annually at the park for a number of years, the highlight being the 50th anniversary celebrations of the Civil War (1911–1915) in which the veterans reenacted famous Civil War battles.

One of the nation's most famous composer/conductors, Victor Herbert, came to Willow Grove Park for the first time in 1902. Herbert, standing in the center holding a cane, is pictured in 1902 with the Pittsburgh Orchestra on the back steps of the music shell. Born in Dublin, Ireland, in 1859, Herbert studied at the Stuttgart Conservatory where he became an accomplished cellist. He came to America in 1886 and was principal cellist with the Metropolitan Opera Orchestra. He began his conducting career with the 22nd New York Regiment Band in 1893 and then was conductor of the Pittsburgh Symphony from 1898 to 1904. He left Pittsburgh to form his own orchestra and to write musicals for Broadway, of which he wrote nearly 50. Among his best-known works are *Babes in Toyland* (1903) and *Naughty Marietta* (1910). He also wrote orchestral music and two operas. Herbert's *Whispering Willows* was composed in 1915 and dedicated to the patrons of the park. Beloved by Willow Grove Park audiences, Herbert and his orchestra appeared second only to Sousa and his band over the years at Willow Grove.

One of the rarer appearances at Willow Grove Park during the nearly 30 years of public concerts was by Helen May Butler and her Ladies' Military Band. During the 1903 and 1904 seasons, park management experimented with bringing in various groups for one-week-only stints. By 1905, fewer groups with longer runs became the norm. Other groups that had minor runs at Willow Grove included Jean M. Missud directing the Salem Cadet Band, A. F. Pinto leading the Boys' New York Symphony Orchestra, the Haskell Indian Band under the direction of Dennis Wheelock, the U.S. Naval Academy Band with Charles A. Zimmerman conducting, and Handel V. Phasey conducting the British Guards Band.

Thursday, July 7th, 1904

OFFICIAL PROGRAMME CONCERTS
WILLOW GROVE PARK

BUTLER

Concerts Afternoon and Evening

BY THE LADIES' MILITARY BAND

HELEN MAY BUTLER, Directress.

Patrick Conway, director of the Ithaca Band, was another one of the great bandleaders to perform regularly at Willow Grove beginning in 1903. Conway and the band were known especially for their performances of the light forms of music, including ragtime, cakewalks, humoresques, and marches. Like many of the other conductors, Conway patronized the park's photograph gallery and is pictured here in June 1910.

53

The Biograph Theatre was renamed the Willow Graph Theatre in 1901. In 1903, the building was expanded with the addition of two wings that increased the seating capacity to 800. As the nascent movie industry developed, the programming at the theater became more sophisticated. The theater stopped showing movies after the 1926 season. The crowds in front of the theater are watching a sheep-herding demonstration complete with sheep, dogs, and handlers.

In 1903, a new roller coaster ride was built on the site of the short-lived Fairy Theatre. The Saint Nicholas Colliery (also known as the Coal Mine) replicated the Saint Nicholas coal mine just outside Mahoney City in Schuylkill County. The ride took passengers through a simulated mine as cars passed realistic exhibitions of miners at work.

A view of the Midway around 1903 shows the amusement section of the park prior to the major changes that would soon come. From left to right, the front of the remodeled Mirror Maze is just discernible, then the Willow Graph Theatre, the Coal Mine, and Ye Olde Mill. At the end is the first carousel.

In 1903, the original ladies' pavilion was replaced by a rather substantial structure that would survive, in part, until the park's closing days. There were wide porches on both the east and west sides with plenty of rocking chairs and tables and chairs.

Also in 1903, a new administration building was erected on the green between the Midway and the music pavilion, due east of the ladies' pavilion. Originally planned as a one-story building, it was completed as a two-story structure in classic brick. The building stood until it was gutted by fire in July 1979, several years after the park had closed.

The interior of the administrative building was designed in the Federal style. The park's management offices were relocated here from the Lodge on Old York Road. A small hospital was also located in the building, and a doctor was available during all public hours.

Three

HEYDAY
1905–1925

In 1902, the major traction companies were consolidated into the Philadelphia Rapid Transit Company (PRT). In essence, this consolidation of the street railcar business formalized the Union Traction Company's monopoly. By controlling the entire Philadelphia streetcar network, the PRT could focus on integrating and filling out its regional network.

In the early years after the park first opened, the traction company acquired the ground between Easton and Davisville Roads south of Moreland Road. The area was used to build a rather substantial terminal, which opened in 1905. The terminal is seen looking northeast across Easton Road.

The terminal handled the trolley cars that came through Glenside (Route 49, replaced in 1929 by Route 6), the lines coming up Old York Road (Routes 24, 55, and 65), and the lines coming down from Doylestown (Route 22) and Hatboro (Route 74). Route numbers were first given in 1911. Passengers disembarked at the terminal on the east side of Easton Road and descended via a ramp into a tunnel that connected with the park underground, on the west side of Easton Road. Looking south, the ramp is visible as it descends underneath the station house.

Looking north, another ramp connecting to the tunnel is visible just along the road. With the new terminal, a great effort was made to keep the movement of large numbers of people as smooth and orderly as possible. Departing trolley locations were well marked, and the timing of departures was controlled down to the second in order to ensure that a crowd of 10,000 or 20,000 people could be taken home swiftly following an evening concert. Park literature stressed that people would not have to rush to catch a trolley following a concert or, worse, leave before a concert was over.

The Tudor-style building for conductors and motormen was located in the center of the terminal yard. Aside from the carbarn, it was the main place for trolley conductors and drivers to wait. Each trolley had a motorman who operated the trolley and a conductor who collected fares and assisted passengers.

On the west side of Easton Road, the tunnel brought people into the park just opposite the back of the music shell. A new concourse was laid out connecting to the Midway; this became known as the Lower or Little Midway. The Flying Machine and the Mountain Scenic Railway, two of the park's most distinctive rides, were built along this route. Just south of the tunnel entrance were a storm pavilion and bicycle shed (built in 1899) and a newly constructed newsstand (built in 1905).

Originally known as Sir Hiram Maxim's Captive Flying Machine, this ride was also known as the Flying Machine or the Willow Grove Air Ships. It was considered unique in the country in 1905 and was modeled on the most popular amusement of the year in the English seaside resort of Blackpool. Its inventor, Sir Maxim, is most famous for his gun silencer—the Maxim gun. The ride stood 100 feet in height. Steel cables connected 10 airships to 10 steel arms. As the structure revolved, the airships would lift up in ever-widening circles. Once at full speed, the airships traveled more than 600 feet with each revolution.

The second major ride to debut in 1905 was the Mountain Scenic Railway, known from 1934 on as the Alps. Designed by John Miller and built by Lamarcus A. Thompson, the railway was built over the former site of Shoot-the-Chutes and a previous coaster ride that operated from 1903 to 1904. Passenger cars rode on trainlike wheels. Two brakemen rode on each train to control the speed and ensure that the train never left the tracks. The cars rushed over raging torrents, past rocky crags, through grottoes, and over hills and dales.

The Mountain Scenic was the longest coaster ride in the country and was the first major ride based on gravity drops. The track was 2.5 miles long and extended south from the mountain to a second building known as the Scenic Palace. Within the Scenic Palace were scenes from nature and foreign places.

In 1906, the original Morris carousel was removed and in its place a new one was installed, built by the Philadelphia Toboggan Company (PTC). The carousel building was also remodeled and the heavy, wooden-shingled exterior supports were removed and replaced with white columns, creating a much more open and airy feel. The carousel was run on a concession basis, with the PRT and the PTC sharing the profits. Music played by the carousel's 65-key organ included such popular tunes as "Love Me and the World is Mine," "Cheer up Mary," and "Somebody's Waiting for You."

The carousel (PTC No. CA-011) was a three-row carousel with two inner rows of jumpers. The PTC was formed in 1904 by Chester E. Albright and Henry Auchy as a design and manufacturing firm that produced roller coasters (toboggans) and carousels. The firm also owned White City (or Chestnut Hill) Park in Springfield Township. Renamed Philadelphia Toboggan Coasters, Inc., in recent years, the firm is still in operation and is based in Hatfield.

Prior to 1940, the park did not run a Ferris wheel ride except for the 1906 season. In 1904, Evan Kimball decided to compete against the park on his farm, which adjoined the park to the west. He secured a Ferris wheel from the Roebling firm in New York (makers of the Brooklyn Bridge). Kimball operated the ride for two years before the park bought him out along with 20 acres of land on a 20-year lease. The Ferris wheel broke down during its first season under park management. When the price to repair the ride was deemed too much, the park illuminated the structure to look like a giant daisy, and it shone forth at night. The Ferris wheel was removed after the 1910 season.

Tours of the World was added in 1906. It was located behind the second carousel and alongside the Mountain Scenic and its Scenic Palace. The ride simulated a train ride. Passengers sat in Pullman cars, and a screen in the front of the car showed pictures of foreign lands. The train cars would move to simulate the rocking motion seen on the screen. The ride, considered both educational and fun, was dismantled after the 1919 season. The building was then converted to a golf game, which operated for two seasons. In 1922, the site became a cafeteria called the Auto Lunch. During the off-seasons, the building was used for receiving. The building remained until around 1950, when it was demolished.

In 1907, a massive water ride known as Venice opened. The building contract had been awarded the previous December to Frank T. Maguire. The plans were by architects Watson and Huckel. The building was a two-story structure of steel and concrete, measuring 225 feet by 150 feet. The ride cost over $100,000 to build.

The main level of Venice contained a series of canals with numerous bridges and careful facsimiles of the Doge's Palace, the Bridge of Sighs, St. Mark's Cathedral, and the Rialto. Gondolas with gondoliers enhanced the atmosphere. During the park's first 30 seasons, Venice was the most successful ride after the Mountain Scenic Railway.

Candyland was constructed at the end of the Midway between Ye Olde Mill and the first carousel in 1902. Within the pavilion, men could be seen making candy and preparing dainty popcorn cakes, one of the park's specialties. For the 1909 season, the building was demolished and a new Candyland was built on ground just opposite, at the inside corner of the Midway and the Upper Midway.

In order to make room on the Midway for Venice, the photograph gallery and the Mirror Maze (left) were relocated to the Little Midway alongside the airships. The photograph gallery was originally built around 1903 and was located next to the second carousel on the Midway. Inside the gallery was a studio where patrons had their portrait taken. The portrait was then produced on a postcard. The exterior of the Mirror Maze had been remodeled in 1901.

Air Ship Flight, Willow Grove Park.

This 1907 overview of the park looking southeast shows the ladies' pavilion in the center left and the Midway amusements along the right. The Mountain Scenic is partially obscured by the tree in the center. The airship was the invention of Lincoln Beachey, an aeronaut from Toledo, Ohio, who would become the most spectacular and best-known flyer in the early days of manned flight. Beachey brought his airship to Philadelphia in July 1907. During the Elks Convention in center city Philadelphia, he electrified a crowd of over 500,000 as he flew his airship around the tower at City Hall. He then came to Willow Grove Park and made his first flight on July 21, 1907. He was plagued by heavy winds but was able to successfully maneuver his airship back to base. It was reported that the crowds were "thrilled into silence by the novel sight." He remained at the park through August 3 under contract with management, making an afternoon flight daily during calm weather. His airship was displayed in a large tent on the west side of the park. In San Diego, on November 19, 1913, Beachey became the first pilot to perform the "loop-the-loop." He died in 1915 over the San Francisco Bay while performing aerobatics at the Panama Pacific Exhibition, held in celebration of the opening of the Panama Canal.

For the 1909 season, Ye Olde Mill, Candyland, and the baseball field and grandstand were removed for the Automobile Race Course. The ride remained through the 1915 season and capitalized on the new and growing interest in automobiles.

The racecourse featured full-sized cars that sped along four parallel tracks on a fairly substantial course layout. The course occupied the ground of the old bicycle track. Just to the west of the Automobile Race Course was the Nickel Scenic to which the PTC did reconstruction work (PTC No. RC-013) also in 1909.

After the 1909 season, the original Dentzel Carousel in the second carousel building was removed. Thomas Ryan was awarded the concession. He installed an M. C. Illions and Sons Carousell Works machine that he purchased from Coney Island. It was a four-row carousel that would remain at the park until it closed. The carousel was then purchased by collector Charlotte Dinger, who displayed it at her Carousel World Museum in Peddler's Village in Lahaska. Following her death in 1997, the merry-go-round was dismantled and sold.

Also in 1909, a large food pavilion was built along the Little Midway across from the airships. The building would stand as an eatery until the final days of the park.

Upstairs in the food pavilion was a café. Initially called the New Café, it was renamed the Japanese Café in 1916, and later, after 1920, the Tokio Café. It included plenty of room for patrons to dine on white table cloths served by an attentive and well-trained staff.

On the ground floor of the food pavilion was a soda fountain that served a variety of drinks, snacks, and ice cream. Drinks included grenadine lemonade, loganberry punch, and sodas of various flavors, including strawberry, ginger, red orange, raspberry, grape, pineapple, peach, lemon, and sarsaparilla.

6-16-05 2022

In addition to well-known groups who performed at Willow Grove, a number of local choirs, soloists, and other musical ensembles had their day at the park, either providing short musical performances or augmenting the main concerts. The Strawbridge and Clothier Chorus, accompanied by Victor Herbert's Orchestra and under the direction of Herbert J. Tily, performed the afternoon concert on June 16, 1905. Tily was director of the chorus and manager of Strawbridge's Philadelphia store. The chorus appeared annually at the park beginning in 1905 and performed various major choral works over the years. Beginning in 1913, the park removed a section of the public benches in front of the stage and installed more comfortable seating for which there was a charge. The concerts were still free, but there was a price for the nicer seats.

The PRT promoted the park concerts throughout the region. Posters were designed and placed on trolley cars and on billboards. This poster design touts Sousa's appearance at the park in 1906. A goddess on a winged wheel rides over the earth holding out a framed portrait of Sousa. Who then could pass up the opportunity to see Sousa at Willow Grove Park? Sousa and his band were not only the most popular ensemble to perform at the park but also the highest paid at $7,000 per week (the norm was between $3,000 and $4,000 per week).

Each band or orchestra that appeared at the park was contracted for and paid on a weekly basis. Typically the conductor was responsible for assembling an ensemble and seeing to it that the men were paid. For the week of May 30, 1908, Arthur Pryor was paid $3,000. His signature is at the bottom of the receipt.

Since the park's inception, performers and patrons who came to Willow Grove for more than one day relied upon the inns and boardinghouses that sprang up around the park. The Hotel Phoenix was one of the early hotels. Located on the south side of what is now Berrell Avenue, the Phoenix overlooked the trolley terminal. It was built in late 1904 by R. J. Wells on the plans of architect Peter Kuhn. Originally named the Evergreen Inn, it burned in March 1905 and was quickly rebuilt as the Hotel Phoenix. The building no longer remains.

In 1901, J. Catherwood Robinson built the Parkside Boarding House on Park Avenue just north of Moreland Road. The house had a restaurant on the ground floor and 40 rooms on the upper floors. The building still stands, serving now as an apartment building. It originally was surrounded by a large lawn and flower gardens.

72

On the very southern side of the park along Old Welsh Road was the freight house. The building was located on the rail loop that circled the park. Behind the freight house across the street stood the Highland, another lodging establishment. The building still stands on the corner of Arnold Avenue, although the low restaurant wing no longer remains.

In addition to established facilities built for the hospitality trade, others converted their homes to accommodate the summer visitors. This home, which no longer stands, was located on Old Welsh Road next to the Highland. The establishment aimed to please by quick service for lunch or dinner.

In 1911, another one of the park's major roller coaster rides was unveiled. The Giant Racing Coaster (also known as the Race to the Clouds or the Chase through the Clouds) was constructed near the Scenic Railway and the first carousel along a concourse that became known as the Upper Midway. The coaster was a side-friction coaster made up of two intertwining tracks along which two cars raced each other. The Giant Racing Coaster was one of the largest along the East Coast.

The support structure for the Giant Racing Coaster was a giant latticework of wooden supports and trusses. The ride was constructed by A. Jarvis and Coaster Construction Company. Sometime after the 1930 or 1931 season, the ride was removed. The front façade was retained for a show ground that opened in 1932.

The view on July 30, 1914, from the top of the Giant Racing Coaster across the grounds of the park provides a nice overview of the developing park. In 1902, there were only a few buildings on the south side of the casino, but by 1914, the focus of the park had clearly shifted. Between the Giant Racing Coaster and the Mountain Scenic Railway lie the ladies' pavilion and the administrative building. To the left, the path leading past the rear of the casino heads toward the food pavilion and the airships ride. Behind and on the hill is the Hotel Phoenix on Berrell Avenue. To the right of the Mountain Scenic along the Midway is the second carousel and Venice. Around 1910, a new front façade was added to the carousel building and Venice was repainted in a dark color. Out of view to the right continuing along the Midway are the Willow Graph Theatre, the Coal Mine, the Automobile Race Course, the first carousel and the Nickel Scenic. On the inside corner of the Midway and the Upper Midway stands Candyland.

Construction of the Miniature Railway is nearing completion in this late June 1911 photograph. The railway was built next to the Giant Racing Coaster on the Upper Midway. The railway track went under the Giant Racing Coaster with a terminus on the opposite side of the towering ride. Under various names and over various courses, the Miniature Railway would survive to the latter days of the park.

As seen in 1916, on the south side of the Giant Racing Coaster was a shooting gallery in addition to the terminus of the Miniature Railway and the Whip. The corner of the entrance to the Nickel Scenic is visible to the far left. The scale of the Giant Racing Coaster is apparent in comparison to the other buildings along its side.

In addition to the Giant Racing Coaster, a scenic railway was added to the Coal Mine in 1911. The name of the ride was changed to Coal Mine and Additional Scenic Ride.

The track work of the Coal Mine's scenic ride extended behind the building toward the southern end of the park. The ride would remain until it was replaced in 1928 by the Thunderbolt.

For the 1916 season the Automobile Race Course was eliminated. The tracks were removed and the entrance building was converted into Dance Land. The building hosted live dancing where one could pay 10¢ a couple for one dance or 5¢ per person to sit in the balcony and watch the proceedings.

Inside, Dance Land consisted of a massive ballroom surrounded by a balcony. Gentlemen were not allowed in without being accompanied by at least one lady. Live music was provided, and there were various dancing highlights throughout the week, including the novelty dance on Wednesdays, the surprise dance on Thursdays, and a dancing contest with prizes awarded on Fridays. There was no dancing on Sundays.

In 1916, a fun house named Crazy Village was built in between Dance Land and the first carousel. Designed, built, and owned by the PTC, Crazy Village operated on a concession basis with various operators over the years. The original structure had a much less interesting and grimmer façade than the one pictured here in 1920. In 1927, the PTC held fire insurance on the building totaling $17,000 aggregated from 16 different insurance carriers.

Inside Crazy Village was a small village square. Windows and doors were trick and misaligned, signs were misspelled, and the clock was also mixed up. People would walk through the street and its buildings where other fun house tricks awaited. This view from 1916 shows the original configuration. Like the exterior, the interior was remodeled in 1920. After the PTC lease expired in 1928, the park operated the fun house and called it Crazy House. It was removed after the 1933 season.

Also in 1916, the park added a ride called the Whip. It was located alongside the Giant Racing Coaster. Sometime around 1931, the ride was relocated to the Little Midway next to the food pavilion.

In 1919, a new roller coaster called the Forest Ride was designed and built by the PTC (PTC No. RC-027). It was located near the Lakeside Café and extended into the grove of trees behind the first picnic grove. It was operated on a concession basis. As with many of the other rides in the park, the admission price to the Forest Ride included a special war tax. The war tax, which was levied from 1919 through 1921, was a result of World War I.

On Memorial Day 1917, there was a flag-raising ceremony on Old York Road just in front of the PRT carbarn. PRT chairman of the board, Edward T. Stotesbury, was present for the ceremonies along with other distinguished guests, including W. W. Frazier, the Honorable Charles A. Ambler, the Honorable Henry W. Watson, and the Honorable Fletcher W. Stiles. Stotesbury addressed the crowd of school children, soldiers, and other citizens, while what little traffic there was on Old York Road paused to listen. Stotesbury came onto the PTC board in 1910 to oversee the financial affairs of the company at a time when it was on the verge of bankruptcy. Stotesbury was a partner in Drexel and Company and lived in a palatial mansion called Whitemarsh Hall in Springfield Township. He would resign in July 19, 1920, after an unsuccessful fight with company president Thomas E. Mitten over the abolition of the 5¢ fare. During the Stotesbury-Mitten period, the transit company finances were reestablished, making it one of the nation's only large traction concerns not in the hands of receivers. Beyond the gathered crowd, just in view at the far left, is the corner of the Waiting Room where people waiting for the trolley along Old York Road would gather. Looking north, what is now called the Willow Inn is visible on its original site at the divide of Easton and Old York Roads.

On August 7, 1920, N. Snellenburg and Company held its first company picnic and music festival at Willow Grove Park. The Snellenburg Military Band, under the direction of J. A. Carroll, performed as part of the music festival. Snellenburg's was a popular department store at the time, and later in the 1950s, it would occupy a location on former park ground on the north side of Moreland Road. The flag above the stage later hung for a time at the Willow Grove Park Lanes before it was acquired by the Navy League, which had it restored. On April 17, 1985, the restored flag was unveiled at the officers club at the Willow Grove Naval Air Station.

John Philip Sousa and his wife stroll through the park in this c. 1919 photograph. He holds his customary cigar and appears casually dressed compared to the uniform he wore while conducting. As much as park patrons loved Sousa, so Sousa loved his engagements at the park. He maintained a network of friends and acquaintances throughout the area. He also enjoyed the country and his morning horse rides.

Giuseppe Creatore, conductor of the Royal Italian Band, was another one of the musical favorites at Willow Grove Park. Creatore had his conducting start at Willow Grove in 1900. He returned every few years through 1925 and was considered a conducting sensation because of his unorthodox manner of directing. It was said that all of Philadelphia went to see him, half to hear his music and the rest to watch him direct. Beginning in 1920, the park stopped printing daily concert programs and went to a weekly format that was distributed only to paying patrons. While many still attended the concerts, the days of live music at the park were on the decline.

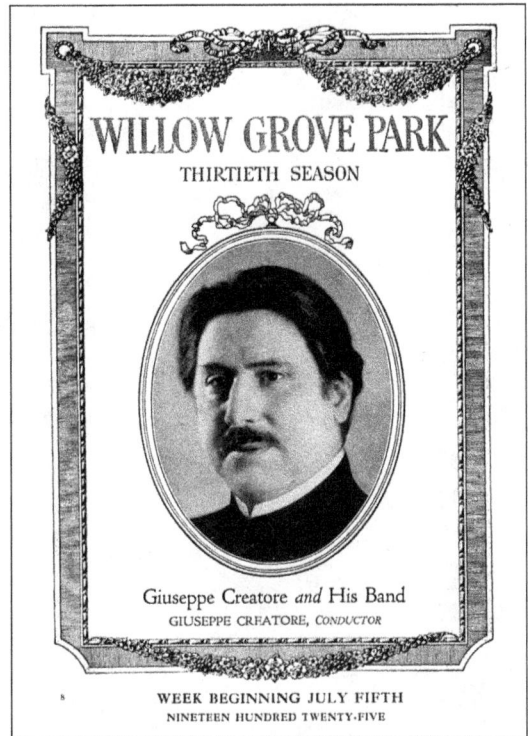

WILLOW GROVE PARK
THIRTIETH SEASON

Giuseppe Creatore *and* His Band
GIUSEPPE CREATORE, CONDUCTOR

WEEK BEGINNING JULY FIFTH
NINETEEN HUNDRED TWENTY-FIVE

In 1922, the PTC removed its carousel from the first carousel building, rebuilt it as No. CA-068R, and installed it in Cape May, New Jersey. In its place, the PTC installed a three-row carousel originally built for Ocean Grove, New Jersey, but never delivered (PTC No. CA-063). In 1927, this carousel was removed and sent to the Chain of Rocks Fun Fair in St. Louis, Missouri, where it remained until it burned in a fire in 1977. After 1927, with the removal of the PTC carousel, the park would only have one carousel located in the second carousel building by the Mountain Scenic. The first carousel building was converted into a shelter for the Tilt-A-Whirl ride.

An aerial view looking west over Willow Grove Park around 1925 shows the general layout of the park and the surrounding countryside. Easton Road runs left to right, and Moreland Road runs along the right side. The trolley lines coming in from Glenside and along Old York Road are seen along Berrell Road before they turn into the terminal. All of the park's major attractions are clearly visible, including the music pavilion by the lake (with a covered walk to the tunnel), the airships and Mountain Scenic Railway along the Little Midway, the Midway including Venice, the Coal Mine and Additional Scenic Ride, and Dance Land, and the Giant Racing Coaster along the Upper Midway. The Lakeside Café and the Forest Ride are seen beyond the main lake.

Four

INTERLUDE AND REPRISE
1926–1953

In advance of the 1926 season, the PRT entered into a 10-year lease with orchestra leader and promoter Meyer Davis, whereby the park became Davis's. Davis was not in favor of the free public concerts and, as the PRT had already booked the engagements for the year, he charged for admission. The sun had set on the daily concerts. In writing to Edwin Franko Goldman, who had his own band in New York City and had considered touring, Sousa advised him against such a move. The development of the radio and automobile had taken its toll on public interest. While Sousa would perform for one more season at Willow Grove, he would only return for single-night engagements thereafter.

SPECIAL EDITION—ROTARY CLUB DAY, TUESDAY, AUG. 23

Miss Phila.
to be Chosen
at
Willow Grove
Aug. 9

WILLOW GROVE
ILLUSTRATED NEWS

Health, Fun
Recreation
For the Youth
of America

VOL. 2, NO. 13   PHILADELPHIA, SATURDAY, AUGUST 6, 1927   FREE TO PATRONS

TO LOOK LIKE PRINCESS
SATURDAY BAND PROGRAM ON PAGE FOUR   STORY ON PAGE THREE

VINCENT LOPEZ AND BAND SUNDAY
STORY AND PROGRAM ON PAGE SEVEN

"MISS PHILADELPHIA"

PERHAPS THIS IS YOU

1927

MISS PHILADELPHIA'S PICTURE WILL BE IN UPPER CIRCLE IN NEXT WEEK'S ISSUE

JUDGE
SPEAKS:

"You will be judged for more than mere beauty of face and figure. Miss Philadelphia will have charm, grace and personality plus natural beauty. She may be blonde, brunette or red-head, curled or bobbed. The artists who comprise the board of judges will look for a girl fit, indeed, to be Miss Philadelphia."
—VICTOR GUINNESS, Chairman.

Meyer Davis had made a name for himself at a young age in Washington, D.C., as an orchestra leader for society dances. He developed the concept of a dance orchestra where all the arrangements were fully written out. His meticulous arranging allowed him to organize several orchestras, all of which carried the Meyer Davis name. Davis brought an enormous energy to the park that was only outdone by his ability as a promoter. He instituted a weekly *Willow Grove Illustrated News*, which featured happenings at the park. The somewhat staid management of the PRT gave way to the excess of the Roaring Twenties as Davis staged beauty pageants, leg and ankle contests, and other racy spectacles. Hollywood stars and other well-known performers of the day were brought to the park to either perform or make an appearance. Davis sought to create excitement about the park and to include something for everyone. Many visitors no longer came by trolley car but by automobile. Those who drove were given park coupons and a chance to win cash prizes. Several new rides were added, including the Tumble Bug, Over-the-Jumps, Custer Cars, Hey Dey, and the Coney Racer. In 1926, the lake was given over every afternoon at 3:30 p.m. to the Willow Grove Athletic Club for water sports. In 1927, the former Miniature Railway was rerouted to circle the park and was renamed the Midget Railway. In 1928, the thrilling Thunderbolt roller coaster ride debuted; it would remain until the park closed.

On December 20, 1929, fire broke out in the machine shop located at the rear of the old Willow Graph Theatre. Twenty local fire companies responded to the blaze. The inferno consumed Venice and the old theater, which had been used for Whirl-O-Ball since 1927. The Thunderbolt coaster suffered minor damage, as did the carousel. A portion of the Mountain Scenic also caught fire. There were no deaths or serious injuries. The disastrous effects of the fire required a large investment in order to rebuild. This, along with the Depression, led Davis to terminate his lease with the PRT by the end of 1930.

James Michener's novel *The Fires of Spring* (1949) reflected, in part, his own experiences while working at Willow Grove Park in the summers of his high school years. Michener grew up in Doylestown and later attended Swarthmore College (class of 1929). He worked at the park during the later days of the PRT. However, the air of decadence portrayed in his novel and the fictitious scene of a great fire taking several lives echo the cheap promotionalism of the Davis management and the 1929 fire (without the loss of life).

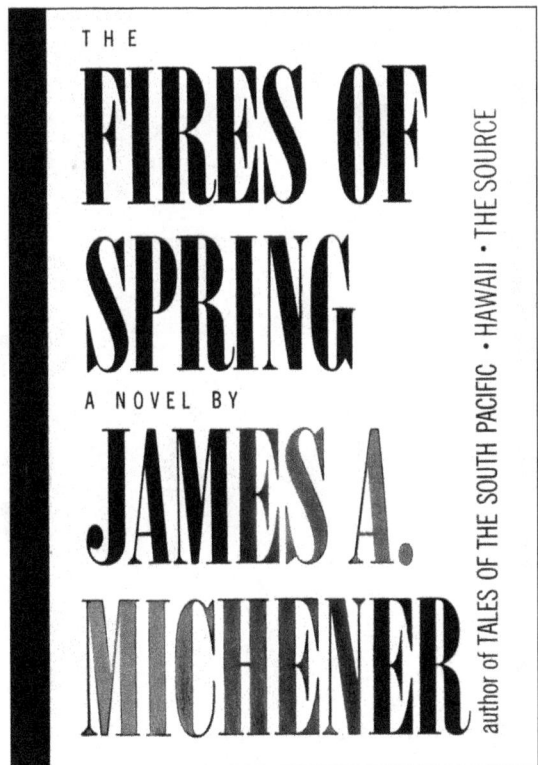

THE

FIRES OF

SPRING

A NOVEL BY

JAMES A.

MICHENER

author of TALES OF THE SOUTH PACIFIC · HAWAII · THE SOURCE

On April 16, 1931, the park reopened under PRT management. Beginning on November 24, 1931, the park played host to a dance marathon. WPEN broadcast the marathon every night at 8:30 p.m. After dancing for 160 hours, the marathon dancers took time to pose in the old casino building. A dancing craze had overtaken the country during the early days of the Depression, and Willow Grove Park was not immune.

For the beginning of the 1932 season, the Giant Racing Coaster was dismantled, and the area behind the front entry gates was turned into a large rodeo ring. Various acts came to the park to perform. In 1932, California Frank's rodeo opened on Memorial Day and entertained patrons for the season. Frank is seen here with a group of Sioux Indians.

COWGIRLS WITH BUCK TAYLORS RODEO, WILLOW GROVE PARK, PA. (DOUBLEDAY)

California Frank's codirector, Col. Buck Taylor, returned in 1933 with his own Wild West show. The original Buck Taylor was William Levi Taylor, a cowboy who attracted the attention of Prentiss Ingraham, who wrote a dime novel entitled *Buck Taylor, King of the Cowboys* (1887). The book had the effect of romanticizing the figure of the cowboy and turning him into an American icon. William F. "Buffalo Bill" Cody, not wasting an opportunity, soon devised a Wild West show that toured the country and featured Buck Taylor.

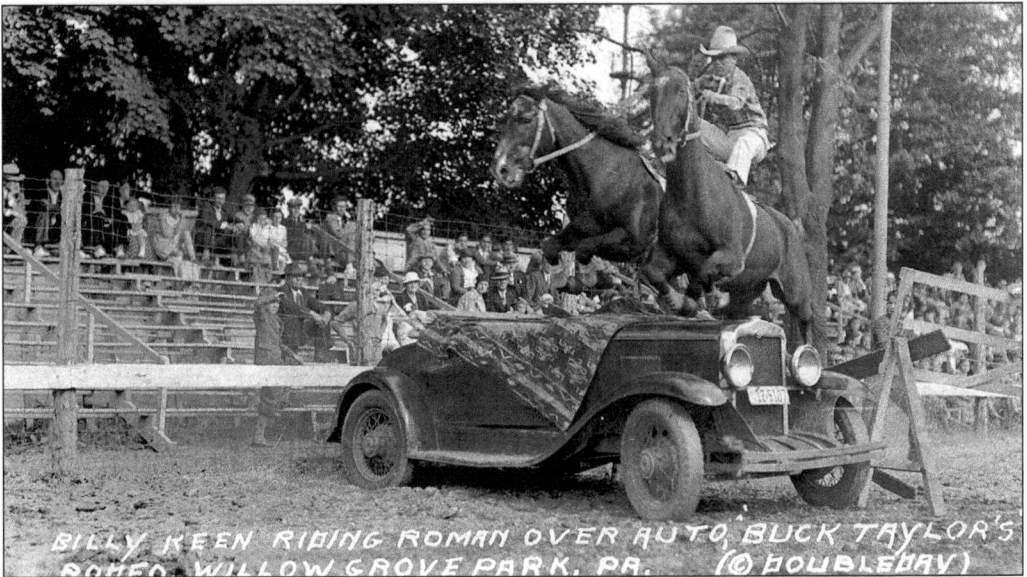

BILLY KEEN RIDING ROMAN OVER AUTO, BUCK TAYLOR'S RODEO, WILLOW GROVE PARK, PA. (© DOUBLEDAY)

The original Buck Taylor left Cody in 1894 to form his own Wild West show, which did not fare so well. It folded and, coincidentally, Taylor resettled to Betzwood Farm in Montgomery County. He lived on various farms in Pennsylvania for the rest of his life, eventually dying in West Chester on April 28, 1924. However, the name of Buck Taylor lived on. Several people either adopted the name or were actually named Buck Taylor, including an actor who appeared on the television show *Gunsmoke* and Willow Grove Park's own Col. Buck Taylor. Colonel Taylor and his troupe would return for the 1934 season.

Beginning in 1915, the park annually hosted the Volunteer Firemen's Association of Montgomery County. The day included demonstrations and contests as well as a parade. In 1931, the parade made its way down the Midway. The large roller coaster to the left is the Thunderbolt. Coming down the Midway was an arcade and the Water Scooters.

The Firemen's Association was founded on January 21, 1909, in Jenkintown to better coordinate cooperation among independent fire companies in the area. Sousa was to have written and dedicated a march entitled "The Volunteer Firemen" in 1924 to the association but never did. The parade of fire engines coming up the Midway was an impressive sight.

Over the years, other fire company associations also met at Willow Grove Park. On September 2, 1939, fire companies competed at the annual outing of the Bucks and Montgomery Counties volunteer firemen. Pumping contests usually included one event where teams raced to see who could have water come out of the nozzle first after having fully laid out 200 feet of hose. Other events included a hose contest and a ladder and hose contest.

In 1941, the Abington Fire Company proudly displays the Abington Township Firemen's Association trophy that reads, "Willow Grove Park Abington Township Firemen's Contest Perpetual Trophy." Fire company events would remain one of the great traditions of Willow Grove Park.

Sometime around 1930, the electric fountain fell into disrepair and was later rendered inoperable. In 1934, the PRT rebuilt the fountain as part of its program to overhaul the park and named it the Sousa Memorial Fountain after John Philip Sousa, who had died in 1932. Members of the Sousa family including his widow attended the dedication ceremonies held on Sunday evening, July 1, 1934. The new fountain was built under the direction of Major Darlington on the foundation of the old fountain, which he also built.

The Sousa Memorial Fountain was constructed of white concrete and was considerably larger than the first. The inner tier was circular in design with a 50 foot diameter and was 16 feet high; four plinths rose around the center tier. It was primarily intended for night operation and had built-in floodlights, controlled from the fountain house on the lakeside. Pumps were able to force the water more than 100 feet into the air. There were two fountain shows a day, one at 4:00 p.m. and one at 10:00 p.m. Despite being named for Sousa, the fountain was regularly referred to as the Fountain of Rainbows. It was demolished in 1959 when the lake was largely filled in.

In 1939, the casino reopened as a modern ballroom. On opening night, Larry Fotin and his twelve-piece dance orchestra played, accompanied by the "Velvet-Voiced Vocalist." The dance floor claimed to be one of the best in the country. It was made of the finest maple and laid in parquet style. The former Dance Land building on the Midway was converted into a roller-skating rink. Skateland would be the only park amusement that would remain open year-round. On December 27, 1948, Skateland burned down. No new building was erected on the site, but the space was filled with a number of small rides for children, and the area was named Kiddie Land.

In 1934, on the site of Crazy Village, the PTC built a water ride called the Old Mill. In 1937, it was renamed the Lost River. This ride included boats that were propelled by submerged water jets. Inside the covered portion of the ride, boats passed through underground canals depicting various scenes, including a jungle. When Skateland burned in 1948, part of the Lost River was lost, too. The ride was rebuilt and renamed the Tunnel of Love.

After the Giant Racing Coaster was dismantled in the early 1930s, the Whip was relocated to the Little Midway next to the food pavilion, which by now had become fairly well enclosed. The low building behind the Whip was a new addition that contained the skooters, which became one of the park's most popular rides.

In 1917, a small building was added between the airships and the Mountain Scenic for Skee Ball. The building was later changed over to Whirl-O-Ball, as seen in this 1936 photograph.

In 1931 and again in 1934, major work was done on the Mountain Scenic Railway. By 1934, the massive station shelter had been removed and the Scenic Palace taken down, although the track layout had not changed. In 1934, the ride was renamed the Alps. In 1939, the PTC redesigned and rebuilt the track course of the Alps (PTC No. RC-102). It would be the last scenic railway installed in the country.

The 1939 World's Fair in New York heralded a new age in design, one that had been developing over the past decade and was very much different from the Victorian design that held sway at the park. Throughout the 1930s, the PRT transformed the look of many of the rides. The once ornate coasters were replaced with sleek and modern trains. Despite the modern-looking cars, the Alps roller coaster was still controlled by two brakemen on each train. They are visible between cars, centered between the two rows of people.

During the 1930s and 1940s, company picnics and other large reunions were important to the survival of the park. Often the events would be held over one or two days with many organized activities, such as contests, games, and races, taking place in addition to the standard park rides. This aerial view of the park was taken around 1934 on the occasion of the annual PRT company picnic. The Alps and Thunderbolt roller coaster rides are clearly visible, as are the other buildings along the Midway. Between the Midway and the ladies' pavilion was a miniature golf course, which was added in 1930. The rodeo grounds are on the Upper Midway. Also noticeable is the fact that the concourse between the ladies' pavilion and the casino is now full of additional rides and buildings, including Caterpillar, Skooters, Hey Dey, and Leaping Lena. As the park became a place where one went to experience ride after ride, the once open grounds gave way to more and more enticements. Also noticeable are the cars parked on the south side of the Midway rides. While room for automobiles had been available for many years, automobile parking was increasingly important for the survival of the park. The parking entrance was on Old Welsh Road. In 1935, the PRT sold its land south of Old Welsh Road to Abington Township. The property is now Crestmont Park.

A boat ride called Water Skooters opened in 1931 in the footprint of Venice. In 1940, a sleek ocean liner was added as the ride's entrance, and a giant smiling whale was placed down the middle of the waterway. The Water Skooters boats were stored in the whale, which also contained a repair shop. Also in 1940, a Ferris wheel was added to the inside corner of the Little Midway and the Midway. It would remain until the park closed. The Ferris wheel is visible over the ocean liner.

Around 1940, the automobile entrance to the park was relocated from Old Welsh Road to Easton Road. A large vertical entrance sign was added, featuring a clown carrying a bass drum.

One of the great icons of the park in its later years was the Swan Boat. It was built by boat builder Ellsworth W. Trout of Roslyn and premiered in the 1939 season. The great swan was berthed on the main lake along with other smaller boats for rent. After the park closed, the swan boat would be moved to Max Hankin's home on Easton Road, where it was visible on his pond over the years. The boat eventually deteriorated and no longer exists.

Over the years, many of the rides added to the park in the open ground around the ladies' pavilion were of a temporary nature, whereby they could be removed as tastes changed. This view shows one such ride around 1940.

An evening crowd gathered outside the former rodeo grounds entrance on the Upper Midway in the mid-1940s. During the 1930s and 1940s, the PTC brought many popular entertainment and musical acts to the park. Weekend concerts would be followed by a fountain display. The attractions would change frequently to bring people back. An All-Star Revue in the music pavilion is advertised here. In the mid-1930s, the grandstands at the rodeo grounds were removed, and the area was used for various stunt and vaudeville entertainments.

In 1940, the PRT was reorganized and renamed the Philadelphia Transportation Company (PTCo., not be confused with carousel maker PTC). The PTCo. Pipe and Drum band paraded up the Little Midway in 1943 as part of the company's annual picnic and festival. The Whirl-O-Ball had been converted to Pokerino around 1941, and the airships building was walled off with a single entrance and small glass block windows.

During World War II, the park remained open to the public. It served as a place of relaxation for many of the service men and women who were stationed at the Willow Grove Naval Air Station or in Philadelphia at the Naval Ship Yard. In June 1944, two shipmates on leave from action in Italy accompanied by two WAVES (Women Accepted for Volunteer Emergency Service) stationed at the Naval Air Material Center at the shipyard, enjoy a day at the park.

By the 1930s, the airships ride had converted from gondolas to airplanes; by the early 1950s, the planes would give way to rocket ships.

Bluebeard's Palace opened in 1927 and was located on the Little Midway across from the airships and adjoining the administration building. The fun house was a rendition of Bluebeard's Castle. In 1941, it was redesigned and named the Fun House.

Among the features of the fun house were jets of air that blew up through the floor (causing many a skirt to rise), shifting and uneven floors, breakaway seats, a rolling barrel, and several typical fun house horrors and scares. Also included were mirrors that distorted the viewer.

After the trolley along Old York Road was discontinued on September 4, 1940, the need for a large terminal at Willow Grove diminished. Within a few years, the yard was foreshortened, and the building for conductors and motormen was relocated to the end of the turnaround. With the park continuing to focus around the Midway, and with the decline in trolley service, the ground north of Moreland Road was no longer needed.

On March 6, 1946, the Hankin brothers bought the park's 13.5 acres located in Upper Moreland Township. The Hankins were a local family consisting of four brothers (Dr. Samuel, Moe Henry, Perch P., and Max A.) and one sister (Pauline, who married Benjamin R. Shanken). A major shopping mall was planned for the west side of Easton Road, including a Penn Fruit supermarket. The park had used this land in more recent years for one of its two parking lots. This picture, taken at the intersection of Old York and Easton Roads looking south, dates from January 1948, a year before Penn Fruit opened.

Just to the south of the Penn Fruit store, a Snellenburg's store opened in October 1953. Additional shops later opened along the remainder of the block. In 1962, Snellenburg's would become a Lit Brothers. When Lit's went out of business, the department store and Penn Fruit buildings were demolished and smaller stores were built facing away from the street onto the parking lot. The row of stores was known as the Willow Grove Shopping Center.

At the corner of the ground where the former waiting room was located (east side of Easton Road just south of Old York Road), a Gulf Oil station was built. The station opened on April 11, 1947. The site is now a Burger King. Just to the east along Old York Road is the side wall of an A&P grocery store, erected on the site of the carbarn.

In the midst of the Korean War, one of the largest Memorial Day ceremonies in the Philadelphia area was held at Willow Grove Park in 1951. A large contingent of sailors paraded through Willow Grove in advance of a lakeside ceremony held along the music pavilion and around the main lake. A moment of silence was observed honoring the servicemen who had died in the war. A flyover of vintage airplanes out of Willow Grove Naval Air Base added to the impressiveness of the observance.

Five

RENAISSANCE AND DECLINE
1954–1975

By the early 1950s, the park was taking on the essential look that would hold until it closed. Whereas in the past the interior ground surrounded by the midways was essentially open lawn, from the 1940s until the 1970s, this area would gradually be consumed by one ride or amusement after another. This view from the early 1950s looks past the Nickel Scenic, the Tilt-A-Whirl ride housed in the old carousel building, and the Tunnel of Love to the Thunderbolt.

The fun house across the Little Midway from the airship ride (now flying rocket ships) continued in popularity during the early 1950s. The amusement was probably best remembered for Laughing Lulu, whose loud, hearty laugh could not be missed. Occupying the site of the former Mirror Maze was the Laff-in-the-Dark, which had been added in 1930 along the Midway and moved to this location after World War II. Below, the Ferris wheel, the Alps roller coaster, and the entrance to the Water Skooters ringed the lower end of the Midway.

This view up the Midway dates from around 1955. During the early 1950s, the park was averaging one million visitors each season and netting profits over $100,000. Thus, it had been retained by the PTCo. However, on September 2, 1954, the directors of the PTCo. voted to authorize the sale of the park. There were two bidders, the Hankin family being one of them. The winning offer, however, was for $1,905,000 by a syndicate headed by three Philadelphia investors. Plans were announced on September 9 for a $10 million shopping center along Easton and Moreland Roads occupying 35 acres, with parking for 3,000 cars. There were also plans to demolish many of the rides. However, the investors who purchased the park had failed to secure financing. In March 1955, additional investors were sought and found in Ben and Herman Cohen, industrialist brothers from Baltimore who headed the group that owned the Pimlico racetrack. In addition to shopping center plans, the Cohens also planned to keep the park, committing $500,000 for new equipment, new concessions, and new rides. On April 9, the park opened for weekends and after Memorial Day was open daily.

One of the new rides that came to the park in the years following its sale was the Wild Mouse. The ride was located near the former ladies' pavilion where the miniature golf course had been. Competition for new rides was fierce among amusement parks. The plans for the Wild Mouse had been smuggled into America from Germany, and Willow Grove Park was the first to introduce the ride in 1958. Other parks soon followed suit.

The Thunderbolt continued to be one of the most popular rides at the park. Designed by Erwin Vettel, the Thunderbolt was a twister using three-car National Amusement Devices trains with under-wheels to prevent derailments. The roller coaster would normally approach speeds of 70 miles per hour, giving its riders a great thrill . . . and then some.

When the Soviet Union launched Sputnik in October 1957, a public fascination with outer space was ignited. The Satellite, while a standard amusement ride, had a unique and trendy name. The center silver satellite was constructed by Paul Simonetta.

By the late 1950s, the former façade of the Giant Racing Coaster was barely discernible, having been remodeled into a row of food concessions. An airplane ride called Flying Skooters was installed in 1941 and was located between the Midway and the Upper Midway. Also sometime in the 1950s, Candyland, long since a shooting gallery, was demolished for more modern concession stands, including a basketball game.

THE ROTARY CLUB OF WILLOW GROVE

PRESENTS

The United States
NAVY BAND

"THE WORLD'S FINEST"

Cdr. Charles Brendler, USN, Conductor

in a Tribute to the Immortal
JOHN PHILIP SOUSA

Sunday, September 16, 1956

Afternoon and Evening

Willow Grove Park Music Pavilion
WILLOW GROVE, PENNSYLVANIA

On September 16, 1956, the United States Navy Band performed a tribute to Sousa. The concert, sponsored by the Rotary Club of Willow Grove, was the last to be held in the music pavilion. The band shell would remain unused for the next two years and would eventually be demolished in March 1959.

In 1957, additional concession stands were located down the center of the Midway. From management's perspective, the goal was to have people spend money and have a good time doing so. Opportunities for both presented themselves at every turn. As the baby boom generation visited Willow Grove Park, the park operated very successfully. Net profits rose five fold during the last half of the 1950s.

The giant whale at the Water Skooters burned following the 1957 season. Rather than replace it, the area was cleared so that a Mississippi River boat could ply the waters instead. Pictured in July 1959, the boat carries those attending the Abington Memorial Hospital Day at the park. The women's auxiliaries of the hospital organized the annual outing, which was held from 1954 until 1966. After 1966, declining conditions at the park did not permit continuation of the event.

During the 1950s, various performers appeared at Willow Grove Park, including Sally Starr, Bill Haley and his Comets playing "Rock Around the Clock" and "See You Later, Alligator," and Frankie Laine singing "Mule Train" and "Lucky Old Sun." In the 1960s, a combination of music, television, and circus acts would help draw the crowds to the park. Dick Clark's *American Bandstand* broadcast from the park in front of the Fun House on the Little Midway.

At the height of its renaissance, the view across the Midway showed a beehive of activity. Numerous rides lined both sides of the Midway, and concession stands stretched down the middle. In the right foreground is the central ticket-purchasing booth. Prior to 1955, tickets were purchased at a booth at each ride. The system lent itself to abuse whereby ticket sellers and ride operators made money for themselves and shorted the park. In 1955, ticket purchasing was centralized. Within a day of the new system going into effect, a significant number of amusement ride operators quit working for the park.

In comparison to the 1950s renaissance, the Midway, photographed on August 1, 1906, is just on the cusp of its heyday. A comparison of photographs between these two pages reveals quite a difference. From the clothing to the amusements, the concept of what an amusement park should be had dramatically changed. The original carousel building and the crosswalk on the right help orient a comparison of the two images.

On December 1, 1958, the Hankins purchased Willow Grove Park from Cohen's Willow Grove Park Inc. The Hankins announced big plans for both the park and for the area along Moreland Road, which was envisioned as a major shopping area. Shortly after their purchase, the Hankins set out to see Walt Disney in California concerning new rides and attractions. Boarding the plane are, from bottom to top, Samuel Hankin, John Palmieri (superintendent), Joseph Helprin (general manager), and Moe Hankin. Max and Perch Hankin were already in California.

While in California, the Hankins admired the world's largest bowling alley with 112 lanes. Upon returning, major changes were made to the north side of the park, including demolition of the music pavilion, Sousa Memorial Fountain, and the surviving stone portion of the Lakeside Café and filling in the second lake, adding parking, and constructing the Willow Grove Park Lanes. With 116 bowling lanes, the alley was the largest in the world. The lanes opened on August 24, 1961, to claims of being one of the world's most luxurious recreation facilities.

The park's well-known advertising slogan, "Life is a Lark at Willow Grove Park," was developed sometime in the mid-1950s. After the Hankins bought the park, Max Hankin approached his friend composer/arranger Jules Helzner and asked him to put the words to music. The jingle Helzner wrote was used in advertising the park on the radio. A 45-rpm recording was made of the tune. On the flip side was Hankin's ditty about fun house Laughing Lulu entitled, *Lulu at Willow Grove*. The nuns and kids having such a good time at the park in the early 1960s were from the Knights of Columbus orphanages, which, starting in 1925, had an annual day at the park.

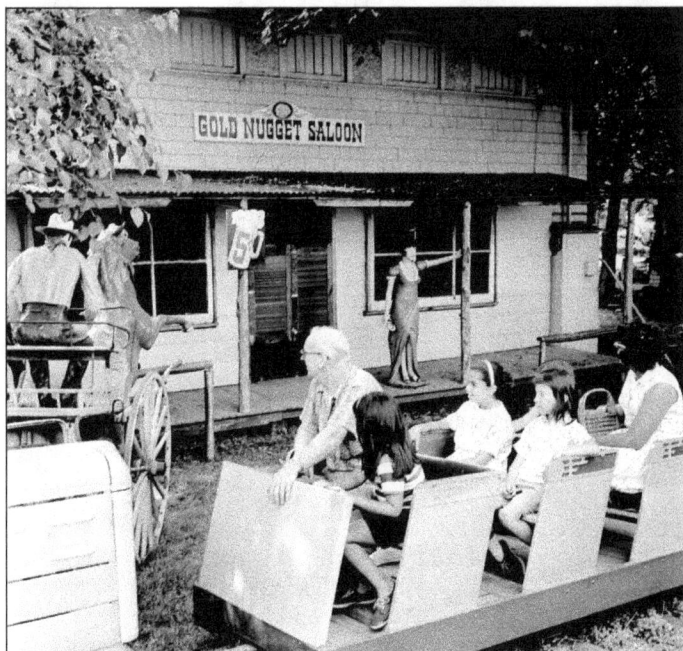

One of the changes made by the Hankins after first taking over was the addition of the Frontier Express in 1960. The Frontier Express was the latest version of the Miniature Railway, traveling across the American West. Passengers rode past a saloon, bison, American Indians on horseback, a horse and wagon, and, in somewhat gruesome fashion, the hanging of a cowboy. Many people would come to remember this and mistakenly think that Willow Grove Park under the Hankins had always been a Western-themed park.

In the early 1960s, the park under Hankin ownership prospered. However, as the decade wore on and attitudes changed, the park had an increasingly difficult time of remaining attractive. For those who wanted the latest in thrills, other parks in the region offered more exciting and newer rides. For others, the park was just no longer a desirable place to go. In 1971, Hankin Enterprises signed a 10-year lease with National Recreational Services, a division of Atlanta-based National Services Industries, to revitalize and operate the park. At the time, National Recreational Services operated five other parks throughout the country. It was estimated that National Recreational Services invested $1 million to rebuild and repair the park in time for the opening on Memorial Day 1972 as Six Gun Territory—Where the West Comes East.

The park no longer operated by charging per ride but simply charged patrons a flat admission fee that covered the cost of all rides. Tickets for adults cost $3.95 and children under 12 cost $2.95. While new features and rides were added, many of the rides remained the same, including the perennially favorite carousel, the one installed by Ryan in 1910 and still going strong.

The centerpiece of the newly renamed theme park was a Wild West town located on a portion of the site of the former rodeo grounds. A town square was fabricated, and character actors staged a bank robbery with a shoot-out for onlookers.

The frontier town also featured the Silver Dollar Saloon, complete with stage, cancan girls, country music, and other Western-style entertainments. No liquor was sold—the park remained dry to the end.

Despite the infusion of new management, a new theme, and new features, the park continued to decline. Emblematic of its waning fortunes, a major fire destroyed the casino on May 23, 1974. Men from the Willow Grove Fire Company fought the blaze along with help from the Roslyn, Edge Hill, Abington, and Weldon companies. Sadly the building had been used in later years for a storage shed. During one month alone in the summer of 1975, the fire company was called three times to the Alps ride to extinguish electrical fires. In August, the Pennsylvania Department of Labor and Industry requested to do a safety inspection of the Thunderbolt, Scenic Railway, and the Alps roller coasters. In October 1975, after "four years of financial failure," National Recreational Services prematurely terminated its 10-year lease for a reported $3 million exit fee.

Six

EPILOGUE
1976–2005

Issues of maintenance and neglect plagued the park. The Hankins talked of a resurrection, but nothing came of it. In April 1976, after requesting the PTC to inspect the major roller coaster rides, the bad news arrived. All three rides needed either a major overhaul or a total rebuilding. For these rides alone, the cost was estimated at $1 million. Within days, the Hankins announced that the park would not reopen. In Six Gun Territory, the Silver Dollar Saloon would host entertainments no more.

A view looking west across Easton Road and down the Midway looked bleak indeed as the Hankins held a going-out-of-business sale. Everything in the park could be had for a price. Coasters, scooters, the Turtle ride, the Wild Mouse, a Giant Slide (next to the former ladies' pavilion), Eli Wheel, Cuddle-Up, the merry-go-round, the Spider, the Scrambler, plus the shops, tools, tables, benches, and any other item in the park were for sale. Once the sale was over, the park would just sit, closed to the passing world.

The Flying Bobs had been installed during the park's waning years. It was built on the site of the airships after a fire had damaged the ride. The famous Twister would eventually be sold.

The Polo Express indeed looked cold and forlorn. In the former building of the park's first carousel, the Tilt-A-Whirl ride was silent and the Tunnel of Love ran dry. Plans to sell the park were announced in 1977. Willow Grove Park was to be sold to Pan American Associates, part of the Ronald I. Rubin organization of Philadelphia. Rubin and joint partner Federated Stores Realty, Inc., announced plans to build a $25 million regional mall in November 1978.

The Thunderbolt, the great thriller at Willow Grove since 1928, stood silent. In time, those rides that were not easily removed awaited their ultimate fate. Meanwhile, in order to gain approval for the mall, lengthy negotiations between the developers and Abington Township began. Neighbors' concerns about the size of the facility eventually forced the developers to reduce the number of planned anchor stores from four to three. In May 1979, the township approved plans for the mall.

The Nickel Scenic was likely the oldest roller coaster in the country still in operation when it closed after the 1975 season. Following the announcement of the planned sale of the park, the Hankin family found itself engulfed in an internal family legal dispute concerning the sale of the park and the other family partnership real-estate holdings. (The total value of all Hankin real-estate holdings in 1978 was nearly $64 million.) After numerous lawsuits, the sale announced in 1977 was made final by a judge on September 10, 1980. The outcome of the Hankins' legal fighting was the court-ordered sale of all family partnership property.

Immediately following the judge's order finalizing the sale, demolition of the remaining park structures began. Within three weeks the site would be cleared so that by the end of September 1980 Willow Grove Park would only be a pleasant memory.

The food pavilion built in 1909 was demolished, while the Thunderbolt thundered one last time as it came crashing to the ground.

The 980,000-square-foot Willow Grove Park Mall opened in August 1982. This view on opening day looks west with Easton Road in the foreground and Old Welsh and Moreland Roads to the left and right, respectively. The mall contained 150 stores and three major upscale anchors, Bloomingdale's, B. Altman and Company, and Abraham and Straus. Overtime the initial upscale polish faded. Sears and Strawbridge and Clothier, the area's traditional department stores, took over the space of Altman's and Abraham and Straus in 1987 and 1988, respectively. Shortly after the mall opened, the Willow Grove Park Lanes closed in June 1983. The facility had been plagued by dampness problems due to underground water and the waterfall lounge since it had opened. As a result of the moisture, the flooring was not satisfactory for professional bowling. The Hankins sold the property to the Rubin organization in April 1984, and thereafter, the building was demolished and a shopping center was constructed on the site.

In 2001, the mall was renovated and a fourth anchor store (Macy's) was added. As part of the renovations, a carousel was also added, thus restoring to the site an amusement that had first been introduced in 1896. The new carousel was made by the Fabricon Carousel Company in Brooklyn. The company was sold in March 2005 and is now known as the Brooklyn Carousel Company.

In 2005, the mall installed several mosaics depicting vintage scenes from the original Willow Grove Park. The works of art, based on familiar photographs and postcards, were designed by Carol Strinton-Broad and executed by the Abington Art Center's Youth Empowerment Program in conjunction with the township's Balanced and Restorative Justice Program. The nostalgia of the original park continues to be evoked to this day.

ACKNOWLEDGMENTS

The Old York Road Historical Society is pleased to once again partner with Arcadia Publishing, and special thanks go to our editor, Erin Vosgien, for her support and flexibility as this work has come to fruition. In the preliminary stages of laying out this book, we explored the option of including other area parks. Even though this did not come to pass, I would like to recognize the cooperation of Edward C. Zwicker IV (president, Springfield Township Historical Society), Debra Wilson, and Howard N. Watson.

In writing a book, one becomes indebted to others who provide knowledge or assistance, which makes the final result not only possible but also a success. I would like to first thank Robert M. Harper for writing the section in chapter 1 about the trolley tour up Old York Road and assisting with the research throughout, Louis Zanine for critiquing the text and sharing his vast knowledge of the park's history, and Joyce Root for reading the text and organizing the images. Others who provided invaluable assistance are Kayla Allen, Lynda E. Benedetto and Anna DiGregorio (general manager and assistant marketing director, respectively, with Willow Grove Park Mall), George R. Haines, Andrew M. Herman, Robert Jordan, Lisa M. and Daniel J. McCormick, Valerie McGhee, John Palmieri, Thomas D. Rebbie (president, Philadelphia Toboggan Coasters, Inc.), Robert Singer, Robert M. Skaler, Elizabeth Smith, Joel Styer, Holly Beth Wilson, and Mildred M. Wintz.

The society is fortunate to have a large Willow Grove Park collection of postcards, photographs, and ephemera. However, the success of compiling a primarily photographic book (as opposed to a postcard book) is due in good measure to two Philadelphia collections, the John Gibb Smith Collection at the Free Library of Philadelphia, which contains over 1,000 photographs of public transit in Philadelphia during the first half of the 20th century, and the Philadelphia Rapid Transit Company collection of over 4,000 glass-plate negatives at the Historical Society of Pennsylvania. Karen Lightner (head of the print and picture department, Free Library of Philadelphia) was most accommodating in facilitating access to the Smith collection. Kerry McLaughlin, Max Moeller, and R. A. Friedman at the Historical Society of Pennsylvania were all quite helpful in realizing access to the Philadelphia Rapid Transit Company collection. Both collections are deserving of much greater study, interpretation, and promotion.

In addition to the society's collection and the two aforementioned collections in Philadelphia, other images were graciously provided by the following individuals and institutions: Salvatore A. Boccuti Aerial Photography in Ambler, George Donahue, Robert M. Harper, Andrew M. Herman, John Palmieri, Philadelphia Toboggan Coasters Inc., Robert M. Skaler, Temple University Urban Archives, Upper Moreland Historical Association, Willow Grove Park Mall, and the Women's Board of Abington Memorial Hospital.

—D. B. R.

Visit us at
arcadiapublishing.com

www.ingramcontent.com/pod-product-compliance
Lightning Source LLC
Chambersburg PA
CBHW050612110426
42813CB00008B/2538